Praise for Birdsong: A Natural History

"Stap has a gift for depicting exotic . . . . A tweet!"

—Natural History

"A lucidly written combination of scientific lore
and vivid reportage . . . a thoughtful treatment
of one of nature's most beguiling phenomena."

—Publisher's Weekly

"This excellent book will challenge readers
to listen to birds as well as watch them."

—Booklist

BIRDSONG

A NATURAL HISTORY

DON STAP

OXFORD
UNIVERSITY PRESS

OXFORD
UNIVERSITY PRESS

Oxford University Press, Inc., publishes works that
further Oxford University's objective of excellence
in research, scholarship, and education.

Oxford   New York
Auckland   Cape Town   Dar es Salaam   Hong Kong   Karachi
Kuala Lumpur   Madrid   Melbourne   Mexico City   Nairobi
New Delhi   Shanghai   Taipei   Toronto

With offices in
Argentina   Austria   Brazil   Chile   Czech Republic   France   Greece
Guatemala   Hungary   Italy   Japan   Poland   Portugal   Singapore
South Korea   Switzerland   Thailand   Turkey   Ukraine   Vietnam

First published by Scribner, an Imprint of Simon & Schuster, Inc.

First issued as an Oxford University Press paperback, 2006
198 Madison Avenue, New York, NY 10016
www.oup.com
ISBN-13: 978-0-19-530901-0
ISBN-10: 0-19-530901-4

Library of Congress Cataloging-in-Publication Data:
Stap, Don.
Birdsong : a natural history / Don Stap.
p. cm.
Includes bibliographical references (p.) and index.
ISBN-13: 978-0-19-530901-0 (pbk.)
ISBN-10: 0-19-530901-4 (pbk.)
1. Birdsongs.
I. Title.
QL698.5.S73 2006
598.159–dc22 2006003492

1 3 5 7 9 10 8 6 4 2

Printed in the United States of America
on acid-free paper

For Benjamin

The best of science doesn't consist of mathematical models and experiments, as textbooks make it seem. Those come later. It springs fresh from a more primitive mode of thought, wherein the hunter's mind weaves ideas from old facts and fresh metaphors and the scrambled crazy images of things recently seen. To move forward is to concoct new patterns of thought, which in turn dictate the design of models and experiments. Easy to say, difficult to achieve.

–E. O. WILSON
The Diversity of Life

One of my favorite images of our small, beautiful world is of morning's first light sweeping around the globe, continuously, relentlessly, forever circling and returning to repeat the cycle. Always, somewhere, it is dawn, and always, somewhere, the birds are singing.

–DON KROODSMA
"Ecological Aspects
of Passerine Song Development"

BIRDSONG

I

S everal years ago on a Sunday afternoon I wandered through the one-story cinder-block building at one of the most famous addresses in bird studies—159 Sapsucker Woods Road: Cornell University's Laboratory of Ornithology. I had been let in, the door locked behind me, and I had the place to myself. To research an article I was writing on bird-song, I planned to review some of the literature in the lab's private library, including materials that were available nowhere else, but within minutes I found myself drawn to another kind of archive. Passing through an unlit hallway hung with the paintings of Louis Agassiz Fuertes, the greatest of bird artists, and an early associate of the lab, I made my way to the southeast wing of the building and opened the gray metal door to Room 125. Stepping inside, I felt a rush of cool, dry air. The windowless room, tightly packed with rows of metal shelves, was austere: white walls, a cement floor, exposed ductwork and girders, and bare lightbulbs hanging from the ceiling. It had the sterile functionality of a hospital room, and it appeared, if anything, cleaner and more orderly. The only sound was air moving through the vents. It would have been difficult to imagine a more lifeless space, yet all around me, stored on wall-to-wall shelves, was the aural life of the planet. This was the archive of the Macaulay Library of Natural

Sounds, the largest collection of its kind in the world. The shelves, which rose above my head, contained more than 130,000 individual recordings, some in neatly labeled boxes containing seven-inch reels of tape, others on standard cassettes in makeshift containers with hand-scribbled labels.

Walking down the narrow aisles, I found boxes that held the sounds of crickets chirping, mountain gorillas thumping their chests, triggerfish squirting water, and prairie dogs barking. It was birdsong, though, that had drawn me there, and birdsong that dominated the Library of Natural Sounds. There, arranged taxonomically from ostrich to raven, were the songs of nearly six thousand of the world's nine thousand or so species of birds. On one shelf were the babbling-brook arias of mockingbirds, on another the flutelike *ee-oo-lay*s of wood thrushes, and on others the wistful melodies of white-throated sparrows, the caroling of robins, and the songs of birds I had never seen nor heard: the superb lyrebird, laughing kookaburra, black-and-gold cotinga, snowy-headed robin chat, and more. If I looked, I could find the sounds of my childhood, the *ok-ka-leee* of a red-winged blackbird and the squeaky-gate call of a blue jay. And somewhere, surely, was Keats's nightingale and Shelley's skylark. The room was brimming with sound. But of course I heard nothing. The silence was profound.

This archive of sounds is invaluable. A second set of recordings made from these originals is kept in a vault in a limestone cave for safekeeping. Several recordings hold the voices of birds now extinct. Many are the only known aural records of rare and elusive species. Recordings like these are critical in one of the newest fields in zoology: bioacoustics, the study of how animals use sound to communicate. In recent years, scientists have discovered that elephants use infrasonic sounds to send messages across great distances; that hippos are able to communicate simultaneously in water and air; that small insects known as treehoppers send vibrations through the stems of plants to communicate with other treehoppers; that vervet monkeys use one kind of alarm call to signal that a leopard is nearby and a different one to signal the presence of a snake. But it is birds that have attracted the most attention. It has always been birdsong that has most enthralled and mystified us. Frogs croak, crickets chirp, wolves howl, and lions roar, but birds *sing*.

Today, many ornithologists are listening to bird vocalizations and studying their intricacies in ways that were beyond the grasp of their predecessors only a generation ago. Avian bioacoustics has flourished in just the last few decades, a result of two inventions from the mid–twentieth century: the tape recorder and the audiospectrograph, or sonograph. The latter, which produces a visual representation of sound, allows ornithologists to measure the details of a bird's song as concretely as Darwin measured the beak of a finch. These tools make it possible to look for answers to some ancient questions: Why do birds sing? What do their songs mean?

Bird "songs"–typically an elaborate series of notes, often musical to our ear–are delivered almost exclusively by the male of the species in the breeding season and sung repeatedly for prolonged periods; in contrast, bird "calls"–relatively simple, brief vocalizations–are made by both males and females to influence behavior in particular contexts (nestlings begging for food or geese honking in flight to coordinate the movement of the flock). Naturalists have long recognized that birds in temperate zones begin singing each spring when they are forming pairs, mating, and rearing young, so the common thinking was that the function of a bird's song was to romance a mate. In the 1930s a series of studies by a British naturalist, H. Eliot Howard, confirmed that birds are territorial. It's now known that a release of hormones, triggered by the lengthening of days during spring, spurs male birds to begin singing to announce their presence to other males. The dueling arias, sometimes punctuated with physical skirmishes, establish territorial boundaries. To females in the vicinity, the same songs (in most cases) brim with that most essential lust: the desire to reproduce oneself. Thus, male birds sing both to claim territory and attract a mate.

But the question is larger than this. Why do birds *sing*? Why have they come to rely on this particular means of communication? One line of thinking connects song with flight. Flying takes a great deal of energy. Song is an energy-efficient way to advertise and defend a territory. A bird need not fly from boundary to boundary to ward off interlopers. It can sit in one spot and sing. There are other ways to ask the question. Why do some birds sing, and others not? Why don't eagles sing like robins? Why does the chestnut-sided warbler sing one song before dawn and switch to another at sunrise? Furthermore, if the functions of birdsong are only to claim a territory and attract a mate, why do chipping sparrows sing one song but marsh wrens sing fifty or more? If both species are equally successful in defending territories and reproducing, what good are those extra forty-nine songs for the marsh wren? Why do mockingbirds continue learning new songs throughout their lives and imitate the songs of other birds? Why in some species—cardinals, Baltimore orioles, rose-breasted grosbeaks, among others—do females sing as well as males?

I left the Lab of Ornithology that Sunday afternoon with more questions than I'd arrived with. A few weeks later, I flew to Cape Cod, boarded the 6:15 ferry to Martha's Vineyard, and followed the winding, hilly roads to Gay Head, on the west edge of the island. I arrived shortly before dusk at a summerhouse overlooking an inlet. University of Massachusetts professor of biology Don Kroodsma had rented it for the weekend and invited me to join him and several biologist friends for what he called, more seriously than not, a party.

With Kroodsma that evening were Jan Ortiz, a naturalist from Amherst; Linda Macaulay, an experienced natural sound recordist; Sylvia Halkin, a professor of biology from Central Connecticut State University; Curtis Marantz, one of Kroodsma's graduate students; and Bruce Byers, who had recently completed a Ph.D. at the University of Massachusetts. Still more of Kroodsma's friends were to arrive the next day.

The "party" began about the time others might be ending–3:30 A.M. I rose, startled by the alarm clock, and turned on the bedside lamp. The house was silent except for a rustling in the kitchen where I found Kroodsma. There was no time for breakfast. Kroodsma was already headed for the front door carrying a backpack over his shoulder. With an efficiency that suggested he was accustomed to getting up at this hour, he quickly loaded up his car with a tape recorder, a parabolic microphone, and a bag filled with cable connectors, batteries, and other electronic gear. We drove off, Kroodsma intent on his mission: to explore the mystery of the song of the black-capped chickadee.

The chickadee is one of the best known and most common birds in North America, a tiny puff of white and gray with a black cap and chin. Its range encompasses the northern half of North America from Nova Scotia to British Columbia, and it is a frequent visitor to bird feeders. Consequently, its song and most common call–a whistled *fee-bee-ee* and a buzzy *chick-a-dee-dee-dee* respectively–are known by even the most casual observers of birds. Yet, many experienced bird-watchers and more than a few ornithologists would have been surprised to know there was any mystery regarding the chickadee's song. Clearly, they hadn't listened to it as closely as Kroodsma had.

Kroodsma, a tall, fit man in his fifties, has been eavesdropping on birds all of his adult life. He is widely regarded as one of the world's experts on birdsong. When I first called him to introduce myself and ask about his work, he quickly invited me to join him on Martha's Vineyard. The mystery of the chickadee's song, he said, was irresistible. I knew the song well, or thought I did, having grown up with it in the Midwest. Of the two whistled notes (*fee* followed by *bee-ee*), the first is delivered at a higher pitch than the second, and the second note is interrupted with a slight hesitation. The tone of the whistled notes and the descending pitch give it a wistful quality. Kroodsma, as hard-nosed as they come when he's thinking as a scientist, becomes wistful himself when he talks of the beauty of a bird's song. Under the spell of the chickadee's modest melody, and mindful that one function of the male chickadee's song is to attract a female, Kroodsma prefers to refer to the song as *hey sweetie* rather than *fee-bee-ee,* as it is often described in field guides.

Nearly every black-capped chickadee in North America, Kroodsma explained to me, sings his simple *hey sweetie* in exactly the same way. This is just what one would expect, I thought. In fact, however, it is highly unusual for a songbird to sing its song precisely the same way across such a wide range. Songbirds, like people, have dialects, Kroodsma said. The song of the common yellowthroat, a rapid *witchity-witchity-witchity-witch,* changes from north to south, each *witchity* containing more "syllables." Dialect differences may also occur in two populations only a few hundred yards apart. The northern parula warbler's song rises rapidly in pitch–*zeeeeeeeeeeeup*. In eastern Daniel Boone National Forest of Kentucky, the ending drops off sharply at the end, while in the west it fades out on a high note. But black-capped chickadees in Montana sing *hey sweetie* just the same as those in Minnesota and Vermont. The conformity is remarkable. Why, Kroodsma wanted to know, don't chickadees develop dialects like other songbirds? He knew of no other species so widespread in its range for which this was the case. The study of song dialects has been one of the most active areas of research in avian bioacoustics. Enough reports have been written on it to fill several volumes, but few had stopped to consider the opposite phenomenon, the lack of variation in the chickadee's song. "Sometimes you can learn a lot about the rule by looking at an exception to it," Kroodsma said.

To put this mystery in perspective, it is important to understand something of avian taxonomy. There are thirty orders of living birds (according to Frank Gill's widely respected text *Ornithology*). While some orders, such as the Sphenisciformes (the penguins of the world), are composed of only a few species, others have many. There are 150 species of Anseriformes (ducks, geese, swans), 288 species of Falconiformes (hawks, eagles, etc.), and 340 species of Psittaciformes (parrots, macaws, lories, and cockatoos). The order of Passeriformes, however, dominates the world, accounting for roughly 5,500 of the planet's 9,000 species. The Passeriformes (small land birds with feet adapted for perching) are divided into two suborders: the oscines and suboscines. The latter, which number about 1,000 species, are found primarily in the New World tropics and are represented in North America by only a few species of flycatchers. But the oscines, speaking in evolutionary terms, are the most successful of all avian taxa, having spread worldwide into a splendid profusion of 4,500-plus species that include jays, crows, chickadees, titmice, wrens, nuthatches, warblers, thrushes, vireos, sparrows, blackbirds, orioles, tanagers, and finches—to name some of the more well-known oscines in North America. It is the oscines we refer to when we speak of "songbirds."

Songbirds are special, Kroodsma told me during our first phone conversation. In the world of avian bioacoustics, songbirds are what all the fuss is about. Although nearly all birds use some form of vocal communication, the widespread development of complex, often musical vocalization has occurred only among the songbirds. Why such singing behavior developed in the oscines and not in the closely related suboscines is one of the great unknowns in ornithology. This is only half the story. Something else separates songbirds from suboscines and the other orders. Nearly all other birds, and every other animal on the planet, are born with their vocalizations genetically encoded, which is to say that they would grow to adulthood and vocalize as others of their species do even if they were born deaf. But baby songbirds learn their songs in much the same way children learn to speak. They listen to an adult, then practice what they hear until they can repeat it. So far as we know, no other land animal—not even our closest relatives, the primates—passes on learned vocalizations this way from generation to generation. Of all other animals, only some cetaceans (whales, dolphins, and other marine mammals in the order Cetacea) appear to learn their "songs"—though the process is not well understood.

Learning increases the possibilities for variation. For nearly every songbird species studied, geographic variation—dialects—exists. Thus, the chickadee's lack of dialects was intriguing. And it was all the more interesting because Kroodsma knew it wasn't the result of some kind of restriction in the song-learning center of the brain. He knew because he had taken a nest of baby chickadees home, raised them, exposed them to more than one song, and watched as they developed several songs. The study actually involved a series of experiments performed by Kroodsma and several colleagues in the late 1980s and early 1990s that proved that male black-capped chickadees exposed to a variety of songs and song-learning situations will learn more than one song. Moreover, young chickadees that were isolated from each other developed different dialects.

So the black-capped chickadee was able to learn more than one song and even appeared predisposed to do so. Not long after he had completed his experiments with the baby chickadees, Kroodsma came across a paper, published in 1958, that reported chickadees on Martha's Vineyard sing both notes of *hey sweetie* on the same frequency. Mainland chickadees sing the second note, the *sweetie,* on a lower frequency. Kroodsma was intrigued by this peculiarity, and on a trip to the Library of Natural Sounds in the fall of 1993, he asked Greg Budney, curator of the library, if he could listen to the library's collection of chickadee songs. Budney knew that a Martha's Vineyard resident, Dolly Minis, had donated recordings of many of the island's birds to the library, and the recordings spanned more than two decades. "When Greg and I listened to the recordings of chickadees from Martha's Vineyard, we looked up at each other in disbelief. The songs were backwards," Kroodsma told me. The Martha's Vineyard chickadees sang not *hey sweetie,* but *sweetie hey.*

"The mystery deepened," Kroodsma said. Understanding how the Martha's Vineyard chickadees sang might, by way of contrast, illuminate the singing habits of the mainland chickadees. Islands make good outdoor laboratories. Their boundaries are sharply defined, and an island the size of Martha's Vineyard could be investigated virtually in its entirety. More important, if the chickadees on the island were isolated from the mainland chickadees, never intermingling, then differences in song might be connected to evolutionary changes in the two separate populations of the species. The scientific literature on chickadees indicates that they are reluctant to cross open water. Perhaps long ago one chickadee on Martha's Vineyard sang the song backward, and others picked up the variation until generation after generation of the island chickadees had learned the backward island song, never having heard a mainland song.

A year after Kroodsma's visit to the Library of Natural Sounds, he drove to Martha's Vineyard, got up before dawn the next day, and drove to the airport in the center of the island. He parked his car, got on his bicycle, and rode along a route that circled much of the island, stopping to tape chickadees along the way. By the end of the day Kroodsma had recordings not only of the *sweetie hey* song he and Budney had listened to, but also two more songs. Some birds sang *sweetie-sweetie,* and still others sang *sosweetie-sweetie.* How could the birds on this island have developed three songs when the chickadees all across mainland North America sang only one song without any variations? Kroodsma's original question—why didn't mainland chickadees have dialects?—led to new questions: Why were there several songs on Martha's Vineyard? How many songs were there altogether? Was there a geographic pattern to them? Kroodsma decided that looking for answers to these questions was a way to approach the mystery of the mainland chickadee's lack of dialects. He would need to gather hundreds of recordings from the island chickadees, as well as recordings of mainland chickadees. He began planning his party.

On the first morning of the party Kroodsma chose to record at Correllus State Forest, near the center of the island. The night before, he had spread out a map of Martha's Vineyard on the kitchen table and, with his recordist friends gathered around, divvied up the island. Golf courses, city parks, and various public land were accessible in most areas, so it was possible to cover much of the island. Residents were warned of the predawn invasion. The island's newspaper carried an article headlined "He's baaaack." The year before, Kroodsma had alarmed residents as he rode his bicycle past their homes in the gray of first light waving what looked like a gun. The police had tracked him down, but discovered he was armed with nothing but a "shotgun" microphone, a wand-shaped mike with a short handle.

Now Kroodsma parked alongside a dirt road at the edge of the forest and shut off the engine. With only the dome light to guide him, he rummaged through the recording equipment in the back of his car. Within minutes he outfitted himself. Over his left shoulder, on a thick, heavily padded strap, he carried a bulky Nagra reel-to-reel tape recorder, nearly the size of a small suitcase. A second strap, tied to Kroodsma's waist, kept it from swinging too much as he moved. Small digital recorders were becoming increasingly reliable, and several models of high-fidelity analog machines used cassettes, but Kroodsma preferred the Nagra because it was dependable and generally unaffected by temperature, humidity, and dust. A cable led from the recorder to an eighteen-inch parabolic microphone—a "microphone system" to be exact, made up of a saucer-shaped dish with a microphone mounted in the center at exactly the point the sound waves converged when reflected from the concave sides of the dish. It functioned like a hand cupped to an ear, gathering sound and funneling it to a receiver. A second cable ran to a pair of headphones, which rested askew on Kroodsma's head like earmuffs. Kroodsma had tucked his pant legs into his socks (ticks carrying Lyme disease had been reported on the island), and he wore several layers of T-shirts and sweatshirts against the cold morning air of early May, and a glove on his right hand, the hand that would hold the cold grip of the parabolic mike. All in all, he looked like a walking satellite dish.

We walked a few paces from the car and stood near the edge of the pine forest. By my internal clock it was the middle of the night. By any clock on Martha's Vineyard it was the middle of the night. There was not a hint of light in the sky. I had enough experience with birds and bird people to expect to get up early, but didn't realize what early meant to Kroodsma. Kroodsma took it as a source of pride that we were out of the house before the others had gotten out of bed. As we stood in the darkness, barely able to see the trees in front of us, we heard only a whip-poor-will, that insistent voice of the night.

I stood quietly, shifting from foot to foot and rubbing my hands to keep warm in the cold night air. Twenty minutes went by without another note of birdsong. Then a towhee sang a few songs—*drink-your-teeee*—and minutes later we heard a few other birds waking up. Swallows twittered, a woodcock emitted his nasal *peent*, several mourning doves cooed. Then a crow called from overhead, and a catbird mewed in the underbrush just as first light began to creep into the sky. Kroodsma was listening carefully, ready to swing his microphone in the direction of the first chickadee song.

Finally, just after first light, a hundred feet or so back in the pines, a chickadee sang. Kroodsma listened, moving the parabolic reflector back and forth, trying to get a fix on the bird's position, but after four repetitions of his song, the bird fell silent. Five minutes later, a second bird sang briefly, then stopped. Last year by this time of the morning the chickadees were singing nearly nonstop. Unfortunately, two days ago a cold front had come through Martha's Vineyard and dumped sleet across the countryside. Dolly Minis, the birder who had recorded Vineyard birds for decades, warned Kroodsma that birds on the island had nearly stopped singing. Moments after the second chickadee fell silent, a third bird started up fifty feet down the path. Kroodsma took off quickly in the direction of the singing chickadee, his long, purposeful strides leaving me behind momentarily. The bird sang loudly and clearly for a couple of minutes, enough time for Kroodsma to zero in on him with the parabolic microphone and tape the song. But what Kroodsma heard surprised him. Last year the birds in the center of the island were all singing *sweetie hey*, leading him to think there might be a geographic pattern to the three songs. But this chickadee's song sounded like *sosweetie-sweetie*. "I don't understand what's going on here," Kroodsma said softly. He looked at the ground. We waited. Kroodsma hoped the bird would resume singing, but after ten minutes, he made three scuff marks in the dirt with the toe of his boot so he could later return and listen again to bird number three. Though the chickadees weren't singing much, they had most likely established territories by now and so this bird would probably remain here. We walked on. The sun was up. A few crows were calling, but the forest was otherwise silent. It was 6:15 A.M. and forty-eight degrees, details that would become part of the data Kroodsma included with his recording of the bird that sang *sosweetie-sweetie.*

For a short while we walked slowly down a lane along the edge of the forest, then retraced our steps. Back at the car, Kroodsma stood quietly for a moment. Perhaps the chickadees were more vocal elsewhere on the island, he said. We got back in the car and drove a few miles east to a Massachusetts Audubon Society preserve near Felix Neck. Here, the forest was hardwoods. Leaves were beginning to bud on some trees, but most were still completely bare. The scene, absent of color, looked like a pencil sketch. We walked a couple of hundred yards down a trail, then Kroodsma stopped at the edge of a clearing. "It's time to cheat a little," he said, taking out a tape recorder small enough to hold in the palm of his hand. In this recorder he had a tape of a chickadee's song. Seconds after Kroodsma played a few songs, four chickadees appeared in the bare branches of saplings a few feet away. The birds flitted about, agitated and curious, looking for their rival. For several minutes the only sound was the buzzy *chick-a-dee-dee-dee* the birds are named for. Then one bird came particularly close and sang one *sweetie hey,* the reversed chickadee song Kroodsma expected. Moments later, all the birds were gone. Chickadees are gregarious, and despite the cold weather it was a bit odd that the birds we'd come across this morning were so reticent. We walked for another half an hour, listening, waiting for chickadees to announce their presence, but with no luck. This first morning of recording was beginning to look bleak.

"Let's go see how Jan is doing," Kroodsma said. Jan Ortiz, the naturalist from Amherst, was recording at a town park in Edgartown on the eastern side of Martha's Vineyard. Kroodsma hoped the birds she recorded were singing *sosweetie-sweetie* since that was the song he'd recorded there last year. When we arrived, Ortiz was standing at the edge of the park, her microphone pointed at the ground. Not a good sign. Not many birds were singing here either, she told Kroodsma, but the birds she had recorded were singing *sosweetie-sweetie*. As we stood talking, Kroodsma rewound the tape on the Nagra. As he did, a strange noise came from the recorder. Opening the cover, he found several feet of tape bunched and tangled where it had slipped off a reel. Given the disappointing results so far this morning, one would expect some frustration to surface, but Kroodsma's face registered little reaction. Jan Ortiz, whose mouth dropped open, seemed more upset. Kroodsma stared at the tangled tape. "Well, I don't think this recorded anything," he said. He slowly rewound the tape by hand. When he was done, he played the reel from the beginning, discovering that he'd only lost a bit of the last recording. A chickadee, hearing the songs, flew into a nearby tree and sang in response. To me, its song sounded like *sweetie-sweetie*. "Hear that?" Kroodsma said. "There's a break in the first note. This is *sosweetie-sweetie*." I shook my head no. The bird sang again, and still I didn't hear the break in the first *sweetie*. It was becoming clearer by the hour that I had never listened closely to birdsong. Kroodsma pointed to the sand at our feet and with the toe of his boot drew what looked roughly like three waves to represent how this bird's song would appear on a sonogram. Seeing the slight break in the first note somehow made it easier for me to listen for it. When the bird came closer yet and sang again, I could now hear what Kroodsma had drawn. *Sosweetie-sweetie,* the chickadee sang.

Moments later, the bird was gone. Kroodsma looked at the

cloudy sky and decided it was time for a break. We climbed into the car and ate granola. It was still early, a bit past 9 A.M., but Kroodsma was beginning to accept that he wasn't going to record many chickadees this morning. He consoled himself with the weather forcast, which predicted a warming trend over the next three days. Still, he wasn't ready to end the morning. Kroodsma decided to experiment with a mist net to see how hard it was to capture a Martha's Vineyard chickadee. A mist net, widely used in ornithological fieldwork, looks something like an oversize badminton net when strung between two poles. The fine, black thread blends in with the background, making it nearly invisible. A bird flies into it and gets its feet tangled in the mesh. Frank Gill, who was arriving the next day, had a permit to capture six chickadees and draw their blood to compare the DNA with those on the mainland. Since the island chickadees were singing differently from their mainland counterparts, they might have significant differences in genetic makeup, particularly if they were isolated from the mainland population. Kroodsma had the net up within a few minutes and had placed his small tape recorder near the base of the net. He stood back as the recorder played chickadee songs. Any male chickadee in the vicinity, hearing these songs, would likely come investigate what he took to be a rival threatening to take over his territory.

In less than a minute a chickadee flew in, landed in one of the saplings, and sat quietly. It flew once from the branch toward the net, but returned within seconds. When the recorder ran out of songs, Kroodsma approached it and rewound the tape to play them again. The chickadee, losing what little interest it appeared to have, disappeared. Nothing was going well. Kroodsma sighed. "In this business it's important to know when you're licked," he said. With that he dismantled the net and loaded everything back into the car. It was a few minutes past 10 A.M. Kroodsma had already spent six hours trying to record chickadees. He had only a few songs on tape, and the best part of the day was over. Given the weather— it was still only in the upper forties—it wasn't likely that Kroodsma would get any more recordings from the laconic chickadees today.

On the ride back, Kroodsma pondered the island chick-adee's song. "What do we know?" he asked. "The mainland chickadee sings only one song, *hey sweetie,* but these Vineyard birds have at least three different songs. There's *sweetie hey, sweetie-sweetie,* and *sosweetie-sweetie.* And then there's this inter-esting thing the mainland birds do—they sing *hey sweetie* on dif-ferent frequencies. They'll sing the song several times on one frequency, then go up the scale a bit and sing more renditions on the new frequency for a while, then switch again to another frequency. But these birds on the island do something else. I've been hearing them sing their song on two different frequencies, a high and low, but nothing in between." Kroodsma paused. "They're trying to tell us something. I just don't know what. Basically we know a lot and we don't know a whole lot."

Back at the house, Kroodsma placed the sonograph he'd brought with him on a folding table and connected his tape recorder to it. He was anxious to see what this morning's songs looked like. The sonograms would reinforce what he felt he already knew about the songs' structure and their frequency. After more than thirty years of listening to birds, Kroodsma could not only hear the most subtle elements in a bird's vocal-ization, but could hold in his memory the slight differences in song between two birds, or two songs of one bird. As a scientist, though, he would not rely on this. The sonograph supplied objective data. It could produce a visual image on a computer screen in real time so that we could see the sonogram as we heard the song. As soon as I saw and heard a few songs simul-taneously, I began to understand what Kroodsma had told me earlier—how important sonograms were to the study of birdsong. The song itself was fleeting, difficult to hold in memory, but I could keep an image in my mind, and that somehow helped me hold the song too. There is nothing original in the observation that we have lost much of our sense of hearing, as well as smell, in favor of our eyesight, but it had never before been so clear. Kroodsma, like a musician, had simply trained his hearing to be as acute as his eyesight.

By the time he began printing out sonograms, the others had returned and were huddled around the table. In the western parts of the island, Bruce Byers recorded birds singing *sweetie-sweetie,* he told Kroodsma, but a few sang *sweetie hey.* Linda Macaulay recorded in the west as well, with similar results. Moving eastward to the west-central area of the island, Sylvia Halkin recorded birds singing *sweetie hey.* In the northeast, Kroodsma's graduate student, Curtis Marantz, found birds singing *sweetie-sweetie* and *sosweetie-sweetie,* the same as Jan Ortiz's birds in the east. A pattern was beginning to appear, though there weren't as yet any defined boundaries, and some songs occurred in overlapping areas. Kroodsma was puzzled, but it was too early to think about results and conclusions. What he most wanted to do at the moment was just look at sonograms. They would conclusively show the structure of the songs. It was always possible for someone to believe they heard one thing, when in fact they heard something else.

For an hour, Kroodsma produced sonograms of the songs he and the others had recorded, and he reluctantly stopped only when everyone else wandered into the kitchen to make sandwiches. There would be no more recording today, so there was plenty of time during the afternoon and evening to look at sonograms and discuss the results, and with that in mind everyone headed off to take naps. When I got up ninety minutes later, Kroodsma was back in the living room producing sonograms. "I couldn't sleep," he said. "I had to go through these tapes while everything was fresh in my mind, while I could still remember what each bird was doing." Not long ago, as part of a study on the song repertoires of sedge wrens, Kroodsma spent four days of a visit to the Falkland Islands recording one individual sedge wren. When he was done, he had ten thousand songs on tape. He is, he admits, "a bit obsessive."

During the afternoon and evening of that first day, Kroodsma continued to produce sonograms. The following day, a Saturday, the weather improved and the chickadees sang far more than they had the first day. Everyone came back with good recordings, including some long samples from individual birds. In the afternoon, I had to leave, but I didn't miss much on the final two days. Both days were cold and windy, worse than the first day of recording, and generally unproductive. During the weekend, six birds were captured and had their blood drawn, which Frank Gill would take with him for a DNA analysis. When the party was over, Kroodsma had nearly two hundred representative samples of the chickadee songs from various parts of the island. The next month, he began analyzing the songs with the help of three students at the University of Massachusetts. He also recorded chickadees in the Amherst area, getting long samplings of several different birds so that he could determine how many different frequencies the mainland chickadees sang *hey sweetie* on. In the fall he sent out an update to all the participants in the project, noting that he had a big box on his desk with analyses of all the chickadee songs from Martha's Vineyard. Furthermore, he had plotted the songs of 199 of the representative songs on a map of Martha's Vineyard. From this, he discussed what he called an "oversimplified" distribution for the songs, which matched what he had expected. He had now settled firmly on the three basic songs—*sweetie hey, sweetie-sweetie,* and *sosweetie-*

sweetie, tossing out a scattering of unusual songs that only one or two birds sang. Since each of the three songs was sung on both a high and a low frequency, he plotted the high-frequency and low-frequency songs separately as if they were different songs altogether. Kroodsma wasn't satisfied. He wanted more songs to strengthen the data, and now that he had thought about it, he wanted songs from the neighboring islands of Chappaquiddick and Nantucket too. Kroodsma made plans to return to Martha's Vineyard in May of 1996, and several of the participants agreed to do the same.

By the following summer, Kroodsma had most of what he'd hoped to get, including recordings of birds from Chappaquiddick and Nantucket, both of which provided surprises. Although only a short stretch of water separates Chappaquiddick from the eastern tip of Martha's Vineyard, the birds sang differently on the smaller island. Most sang a monotonal version of the mainland song, *hey sweetie.* This didn't match anything the birds were doing on Martha's Vineyard. Nantucket, the most isolated of the islands, held birds that sang the typical mainland *hey sweetie* as well as a considerable hodgepodge of other songs. There seemed to be more variation on Nantucket than on Martha's Vineyard, though the latter was twice the size.

Kroodsma spent eighteen months analyzing the new data and writing up the study. In 1999, he published "Geographic Variation in Black-capped Chickadee Songs and Singing Behavior." He had seventeen coauthors, an unusually high number even for the sciences, where papers are frequently coauthored. The paper details the results of analyzing the recordings, noting the different island songs, their distribution, the songs on Nantucket and Chappaquiddick, and how different this is from the mainland black-capped chickadee song. In addition, the report contains the results of the DNA analysis, which showed no substantial difference in the genetic makeup of the island and mainland birds. At the end of the paper where one might expect some conclusions, Kroodsma lists half a page of questions he would like to see answered in subsequent studies, among them: "From whom, where, and how do young males learn their songs? . . . What is the fate of the diverse songs on the offshore islands? How dynamic are their distributions? Will some dialects become extinct and others succeed?"

I had two reactions when I read the study. I thought of the cold mornings and the reluctant chickadees and also the dozen people gathered at the house on Gay Head looking over Kroodsma's shoulder as he reviewed sonograms. None of that was in "Geographic Variation in Black-capped Chickadee Songs and Singing Behavior." The prose of science is dry and to the point. The report was about methods and results, not the miscellaneous enterprise of the fieldwork itself. But the fieldwork *was* the science, I thought. Science was stirring as Kroodsma drove through the predawn darkness at 4 A.M. to a state forest where chickadees might or might not be singing. There was science in the air when he stood listening for chickadees and heard only wind in the pines. And science was tangible when Kroodsma marked the dirt with the toe of his boot at the spot where he recorded the first chickadee.

Most of all, I thought the results of the chickadee study seemed messy. The distribution of the different songs on Martha's Vineyard didn't present a clear pattern. I remembered another research project Kroodsma once told me about. A few years ago, he was interested in why two closely related wrens—the sedge wren and the marsh wren—had such different singing behaviors. Western marsh wrens sing as many as 150 different songs, and neighboring birds share many of the same songs and know each other's singing habits. They engage in what is known as matched countersinging, elaborate displays of one bird matching another's series of songs note for note. Sedge wrens, similar in many ways to their near cousins, do not share songs with their neighbors. Kroodsma theorized that countersinging suits the social fabric of the marsh wrens because they live in stable communities where birds remain neighbors from year to year. Sedge wrens, by contrast, are usually nomadic, moving to a different location each time they breed (typically twice during each breeding season). But what if sedge wrens were sedentary? Would they behave like marsh wrens? It seemed like a purely hypothetical question. "You could clothe and feed sedge wrens and make them comfortable so they would stay in one place for a million years, and that experiment might give you the answer," Kroodsma told me. "But the experiment had already been done for me. In the Falkland Islands, and in places in Costa Rica and Brazil, sedge wrens are not nomadic. I postulated that sedge wrens in those places would behave as marsh wrens do, developing repertoires of identical songs. I went there and found out I was right. It was a jaw-dropping experience!"

The chickadee study offered no such dramatic moment. But Kroodsma seemed happy regardless. He was enthusiastic when I called to ask him about it: "What I find so fascinating is when you look at the maps, you see that the low-frequency version of the *sweetie hey* song covers much of the island. You see it in the west, on Gay Head, throughout the center of the island, and even far to the east in Edgartown. There are a few pockets of the high-frequency *sweetie hey* within the distribution of the low-frequency version. At one point they had to have occurred together, they must have arisen together, and then one was just more successful than the other, for whatever reason. So, messy? Yeah. But I guess I look at it and don't see the mess so much as the cultural transmission of the different songs. The low-frequency *sweetie hey* was successful, and the high-frequency *sweetie-sweetie* was pretty successful too."

I asked about the other songs. "Remember what the island

looked like?" Kroodsma said. "If you stood on the ridge at Gay Head and looked across the island toward the east, you could see how forested the island is. But there's a picture in a book from over a hundred years ago, when the forests had been logged, that looks across the island from Gay Head and there's not a tree in sight. When I saw that picture, I could imagine that there would have been isolated pockets of trees here and there—chickadee habitat—where groups of chickadees were isolated, and so different dialects could have developed. It doesn't take much for dialects to develop in typical songbirds. Any kind of barrier can create dialects, just as long as the birds are far enough apart that they can't hear each other singing. Here's a very simple scenario. We see three different songs, so imagine there were three different pockets of forest that were isolated from each other during the time the island had very few trees on it. The three different dialects developed apart from each other in those pockets, eventually becoming distinctly different songs. When the forest regenerated, the birds from these areas came into contact with each other, and the low-frequency *sweetie hey* dialect swept the island and became the dominant dialect. There's nothing uniform about the distribution of the songs on the island now, but this is how it may have occurred."

Of course, the original mystery remained: Why did the mainland chickadees sing one song without any dialects? Kroodsma seemed no closer to an answer than when he'd started. "What we saw on the islands," he said, "especially on Chappaquiddick, where the birds had a number of songs per individual, together with that earlier study in the lab showing that chickadees would develop three or four songs, made the mainland birds all the more interesting. What we now know about the island birds adds to the evidence that the black-capped chickadee is capable of singing in larger repertoires. But the mainland birds restrict themselves to . . ." Kroodsma paused a moment. "Here's where you have to choose your words very carefully: they restrict themselves to what looks like a single song that they sing on different frequencies. But are our words—what we mean by *song*–limiting how we think about these birds? Maybe every one of these different frequencies on the mainland is—to a chickadee—a different song."

Kroodsma's leap of thought left me blank for a moment. Singing the same song on different frequencies is not what ornithologists think of as singing different songs. Kroodsma was pushing beyond the customary definition of *song*. It was a human definition after all, not a chickadee's. This was sheer speculation of course, Kroodsma said. "Who knows what all this means to a chickadee?" All along I had misunderstood the business of the mystery of the chickadee's song. For Kroodsma the birdsong party was as much about enjoying the mystery as solving it. "I suppose that good research introduces more questions than it answers," he said. "So in that sense, maybe the wren study was a bust, and the chickadee project was something we should run up the flagpole."

The literature on birdsong begins with Aristotle. *Historia Animalium,* his compilation of what was known about animals in the third century BC, includes observations that jibe with our modern understanding of songbird behavior. "In general the birds produce most voice, and with most variety, when they are concerned with mating," he writes, and "a mother nightingale has been observed to give lessons in singing to a young bird." Pliny, who produced the other great ancient text on natural history, *Historia Naturalis,* is less discriminating between fact and fancy, often mixing the two in the same observation: "The birds have several songs each, and not all the same but every bird songs of its own. They compete with one another, and there is clearly an animated rivalry between them; the loser often ends her life by dying, her breath giving out before her song."

For more than one thousand years scholars did little more than repeat what they found in Aristotle and Pliny. It wasn't until the sixteenth century that naturalists began to make their own direct observation of birds. In the early 1700s Baron Ferdinand Adam Pernauer, an Austrian naturalist, wrote, "The blackbirds sometimes call each other, but not with the intention of gathering, but either for inciting each other to fly, or to warn each other, or as a means of threat." Even more interesting were his observations on how birds learn their songs: "One has to consider that a young bird of any species, which neither hears an adult of its kind nor has another young around itself, never will attain its natural song completely, but will sing rather poorly." Bird fanciers, of course, had known for centuries that caged birds would learn other birds' songs as well as music they heard, so Pernauer's observations were not completely new. In 1773, Daines Barrington, a British naturalist, presented to The Royal Society the results of his observations and experiments on birdsong, "a subject that hath never before been scientifically treated," he said. Barrington raised young birds of different species by hand and noted their song-learning behavior, observing that the young birds begin by making imperfect songs that he likened to a child babbling. After ten to eleven months, he noted, the songs assume their proper shape and become fixed.

Still, substantial reports were few and far between. And no one gathered together what was known or established a systematic, ongoing investigation that others could build on. The problems presented by the ephemeral nature of birdsong—here for a second, then gone, resonating only in the hearer's memory—were too great. Naturalists could collect specimens of the birds themselves, and they could describe bird behavior in their journals, but there was no adequate way to document what they heard. As early as 1650, some tried to represent birdsong with musical notation, but the changes in pitch in birdsong do not generally correspond to musical scales. In addition, naturalists who weren't musicians might as well be looking at hieroglyphics as at a bar of music.

Darwin, who explored how animals communicate in *The Expression of the Emotions in Man and Animals,* published in 1872, despaired of ever understanding communication among animals: "The cause of widely different sounds being uttered under different emotions and sensations is a very obscure subject. . . . It is not probable that any precise explanation of the cause or source of each particular sound, under different states of mind, will ever be given." Darwin could not have known that only five years later, in 1877, Thomas Edison would wrap tinfoil around a brass drum and produce the first crude phonograph. A few years later, Edison was using wax discs rather than cylinders, and by 1889 the Edison phonograph found its way to the Leipzig Fair in Germany, where a man by the name of Koch acquired a phonograph and a box of discs to take home to his son, Ludwig. Later that year the precocious eight-year-old Ludwig recorded the song of a caged Indian shama, a member of the thrush family, the first known recorded birdsong.

Ludwig was as interested in animals as he was in his violin. The young boy had his own private zoo and soon he devoted much of his time to recording birds. By the time he was a young man, advances in sound-recording technology made electrical microphones available, and Koch spent more and more of his time experimenting with techniques to record birdsong. He carted the bulky equipment around the country-side in a truck, and on one occasion, unable to drive the truck across a stretch of land, he laid out more than five thousand feet of cable to set the microphone near a singing white-throat. The wax discs that he recorded on were fragile and difficult to work with. It was critical to keep the discs perfectly level during recording, which meant leveling the seven-ton van, a consid-erable problem, and yet more difficult when recording at night. The discs also had to be kept warm, stored at a constant tem-perature before and after use. Koch dared not play them back in the field for fear they'd break. Thus, he never knew what he'd recorded until he got the discs back to the studio, if indeed he got the brittle discs back in one piece. Writing about his early recording experiences decades later, Koch still lamented losing a recording of a marsh warbler when the disc broke on the ride home. His first venture in producing a "sound book" of twenty-five species of birds required 380 discs, 355 of which either broke or contained poor quality recordings.

During the years after World War I, Koch pioneered natural-sound recording in Germany and, later, after fleeing from the Nazis, in Great Britain. At the same time, in the United States, Arthur Allen, who founded Cornell University's ornithology program, began experimenting with the new technology as well. Allen first recorded wild birds in response to a request for help from Fox-Case Movietone Corporation, whose sound engineers had no experience with bird behavior. In May of 1929, Allen met a Movietone truck at 5 A.M. in Ithaca's Stewart Park and recorded the songs of a rose-breasted grosbeak, house wren, and song sparrow, the first recording of wild birds in North America. Allen used motion picture film to record the sound rather than wax discs, and he had to wait for three weeks for the film to be processed. When it was presented as a short entitled "Sounds of Spring" at a theater in Ithaca, Allen and his student Peter Paul Kellogg were thrilled at the possibilities the venture presented, but thought that they'd never be able to afford such an enterprise. The equipment alone cost $30,000. "Recording bird-sounds ourselves was far beyond our wildest dreams," Kellogg later wrote.

Less than a year later their problem was solved. Albert A. Brand, a successful thirty-nine-year-old stockbroker, had sold his seat on the stock exchange only months before the market crashed on October 29, 1929. Enrolling at Cornell to study ornithology, Brand soon became the university's birdsong recording patron and an ardent researcher in the new field. By 1931, Allen, Kellogg, and Brand had recorded forty-one species. "Many of the recordings were barely recognizable above the extraneous noise," Kellogg wrote, "but, even so, it was already the largest collection of birdsongs in the world." In the following months, the three men enlisted some of Cornell's electrical engineers to design new equipment. Then, after the Christmas break of 1931, one of Allen's students returned to school with a copy of *Radio News*. On the cover was a picture of a parabolic reflector being used in a theater to "catch" the voice of an actor onstage. With the help of a Cornell physics professor, Kellogg and the others located several molds of similar reflectors used during World War I to listen for enemy aircraft and produced their own parabolic dish. By 1932, Brand had produced "Bird Songs Recorded from Nature," two twelve-inch, 78 rpm discs that included "twenty-one species of birds and one amphibian."

Birdsongs could now be collected and archived, but another fundamental problem remained. No matter how often one might listen to a recorded song, it was still difficult to examine the characteristics of that song and compare it to others. Consequently, naturalists continued to look for ways to represent birdsongs. In 1935, Aretas Saunders invented a system that employed vertical and horizontal lines to represent the notes of a bird's song, and indicate duration, relative pitch, and loudness. Saunders's method may have been the most intelligible and the most accurate, but it still did not capture the subtleties of birdsong. How, for instance, could Saunders's "musical shorthand," as he called it, register the song of a hermit thrush, which lasts less than two seconds, but (we now know) may contain forty-five to a hundred or more notes, and as many as fifty changes in pitch?

As Saunders and others continued working on the problem, Koch in Great Britian and Allen, Kellogg, and Brand in the United States were building the foundation of their respective archives of birdsong. Nothing seemed to deter them, not even, in Koch's case, imprisonment. Koch, who had worked in the intelligence service in Germany during World War I, was held on the Isle of Man for several months during World War II as an "enemy alien." There he experienced, he said, a "nice spring and summer" and was "up and out in the early-morning hours in the surrounding country of the internment camp, and . . . was able to make a special study of the hooded crow and the herring-gull." Meanwhile, Peter Paul Kellogg worked for the U.S. army in Panama, recording sounds of the Panamanian jungle that the army could use to acclimate marines in the event that they needed to be dropped into Panama at night to protect the Panama Canal. Kellogg was as opportunistic as Koch. "In Panama," he has written, "we took full advantage of our wonderful opportunity to study birds and record their sounds. When we prepared our report, which the Office of Scientific Research and Development published confidentially, we included an album of two, 12-inch, 78 rpm discs of bird, amphibian, mammal, and other sounds of the tropical environment."

In the years following the war, advances in technology brought biologists the two inventions that would revolutionize the study of animal communication: the tape recorder and the audiospectrograph, or sonograph.

Word of the sonograph spread throughout the ornithological community, reaching William Thorpe in England in the late 1940s. Thorpe, an entomologist by training, was studying parasitic wasps in the 1930s and 1940s when he found himself confronted with one of the hot topics of the day: the relationship between instinct and learning in animal behavior. Which actions of an animal are controlled by nature (instinct) and which by nuturing (learning)? Ethology, the examination of how animals behave in their natural environment, was a new science. Konrad Lorenz in Austria was conducting the famous research on imprinting that would earn him a Nobel Prize and recognition as the father of modern ethology. When Thorpe read Lorenz's papers, he became, he wrote, "increasingly absorbed in, and puzzled by, what one may call the 'problem of instinct' and the relation of this to the learning abilities of animals." And he began to think that wasps weren't the best subject for his experiments. "I had been a keen field ornithologist for many years," Thorpe wrote, "and it struck me very forcibly that for the particular work I hoped to do, birds would provide the most promising material. . . . Birds provided on the one hand some of the most striking examples of elaborate instinctive behaviour (as in their display, feeding methods, nest building, etc.), and at the same time they were capable of extraordinary feats of learning . . . in the song birds especially. . . . So I decided that at all costs I must attempt to switch over from entomology to ornithology."

If songbirds learned their songs, as naturalists long believed, did instinct play a role as well? How exactly did the birds learn? When did learning occur? From whom did they learn? Thorpe had met Ludwig Koch and knew that tape recorders were potentially useful tools for such work. More important, he had heard of the Kay Sonagraph. With a machine that could produce detailed images of sound, Thorpe knew he had an opportunity to do something earlier naturalists could not have imagined. In 1950 the only sonograph in England belonged to the National Physics Laboratory, but once Thorpe had seen the machine, he had to have one for himself. He convinced Cambridge not only to buy a Kay Sonagraph but also to establish a special unit on a four-acre site in nearby Madingley to study birdsong. Thorpe had a subject in mind too: the chaffinch, a common, well-known bird of England. Birdwatchers in England knew that the chaffinch displayed regional dialects in its song. In the spring of 1950, Thorpe set out to learn what he could about its song-learning process. He did not load up his recording equipment and take it into the woods, nor sit all day week after week by a chaffinch nest to watch how the young birds responded when they heard adults sing. Instead of going out every day to the chaffinches, Thorpe brought them to him.

Bird fanciers had long raised wild birds in captivity, so there were ample guidelines for keeping baby birds alive and well. There were also models for how to conduct controlled experiments with animals to understand their behavior. Thorpe reasoned that if he kept the birds in soundproof chambers and played recordings of their species songs on a speaker, he could control what sounds they heard and when they heard them and thereby establish with some certainty the basic process by which the chaffinch learned to sing. At the same time, he could make sonograms and document their repertoire, which included up to six different songs.

Within a few months Thorpe was hand-rearing chaffinches at the Madingley Field Station. The study would take several years, but Thorpe was patient and methodical. He took chaffinches from the nest at five days old and raised each in isolation from all other birds so that they heard no avian vocalizations of any kind. When they produced their own songs the following spring, the songs were simplified versions of the chaffinch song—roughly the right length and right number of notes, but otherwise off the mark in various ways (notes on the wrong pitch, or incomplete, for instance). If the birds depended entirely on learning to sing their songs, they would not have been able to sing even these crude chaffinch songs, so this suggested that the ingredients of the song and the rough outline of it were innate, but the finer details were learned. Next, to determine how much social interaction affected song-learning, Thorpe hand-reared a group of young chaffinches together in the same cage, keeping them isolated from all other birds, but allowing them to interact and hear each other when they first began to sing. This time, the birds developed songs that were more complex than the simplified songs of those birds raised in individual isolation, though they were still abnormal. Thorpe also noted that the songs of the birds in the group were similar in some of the fine details. Social interaction, then, affected the process. Thorpe designed a third experiment to give an indication of how old a chaffinch was when it learned to sing. Rather than taking birds from the nest when they were only a few days old, Thorpe caught chaffinches in the autumn of their first year. Consequently, these birds had heard their species song in the wild, though none had yet developed its own song. Thorpe isolated them individually from all bird sounds, but by the following spring they developed fairly normal chaffinch songs. Apparently, part of the learning process took place early in the chaffinch's life long before it tried to sing. This meant that the birds were memorizing details of the song from adults and storing those details in the brain.

One might have performed these same experiments a century earlier, but Thorpe's observations about the chaffinch songs were based not just on what he heard but on the sonograms he made. The sonograms provided concrete evidence of the abnormalities in the songs of the birds that had been isolated. Thorpe could place a sonogram of an abnormal song next to a normal chaffinch song and see exactly how it resembled a proper song and how it deviated from it. This was the empirical evidence science demanded. In addition, Thorpe's simple, well-designed experiments provided a model for those who followed. Raising birds by hand in soundproof chambers and playing recorded songs to them would become the accepted methodology to study song-learning.

Thorpe was not alone during those first years at the Madingley Field Station. In the late 1940s, Peter Marler, a young graduate student at University College London, was conducting research on plant ecology in the Lake District. "I spent long hours drilling mud cores in the postglacial deposits of the Esthwaite Water bogs and subjecting them to chemical analysis," Marler wrote. "Alas, I was less inspired by the chemistry of mud than by the remarkable diversity I found in the song dialects of the chaffinch in the surrounding valleys." Although he completed a Ph.D. in botany and went on to work for The Nature Conservancy, Marler could not stop thinking about the chaffinches. Eventually, he conveyed his feelings to his employer, "and to my astonishment," Marler told me one day over the phone, "they heard my message." The Nature Conservancy sent Marler to Cambridge to work with Thorpe. A somewhat austere man, Thorpe was a bit shy, a little remote, Peter Marler recalled. "He was a complicated person, and a typical Cambridgian. He didn't recognize my Ph.D. from University College London and never called me *Dr.* Marler until I got a Ph.D. from Cambridge." Thorpe was also more than a little aware that his work was the first of its kind. He was edgy, in fact, about his student writing on the same subject. "We had an occasional brush," Marler said. "He had made up his mind early on that birdsong was 'his baby' and he didn't want me to write on it. I had to persuade him to let me use it in my dissertation." Despite the friction, Thorpe gave Marler unlimited access to the audiospectrograph. The spectrograph enabled Marler to document the complete vocal repertoire of the chaffinch and to provide a functional analysis for all of the chaffinch's various vocalizations, the first such study of any animal.

Marler also questioned a basic assertion made by Konrad Lorenz: that animal signals are arbitrary in structure. In other words, the physical traits of a bird's vocalization, whether it is a high-frequency or low-frequency sound, for instance, are happenstance. Marler noticed, however, that both the chaffinch and great tit uttered a high-pitched alarm call that other birds nearby could easily hear but that predators such as hawks found difficult to locate. The quality of the sound—it is high-pitched with an indistinct beginning and ending—seemed perfectly suited for its function: alert nearby birds of danger but not give away the exact location to the predator. Evolution is at work, Marler thought, and he proposed this in a paper. More than thirty years later experiments with hawks and owls proved that Marler was right. Today, birders frequently make casual reference to the ventriloquial nature of the high-pitched alarm calls of small songbirds that confuse a nearby hawk, unaware that this is one of the early discoveries a young bird enthusiast made when little was yet known about birdsong.

After seven years of working in Thorpe's shadow, Peter Marler accepted an offer to teach at the University of California at Berkeley, bringing with him the new field of birdsong studies. In 1957, others in the United States were examining birdsong with the audiospectrograph, but no one else would have as great an impact on avian bioacoustics as Marler. A man with a sharp mind and an ability to synthesize ideas from his wide-ranging interests (on his first sabbatical at Berkeley he went to Africa to study vocalizations in monkeys, working for a time with Jane Goodall), Marler is widely considered to be the father of North American avian bioacoustics. His early work at Berkeley on the white-crowned sparrow is probably the most-cited paper in the literature, and it led to so much subsequent research that the bird has been studied more than any other songbird on the continent.

The white-crowned sparrow *(Zonotrichia leucophrys),* which ranges widely across North America, has a distinctive black-and-white cap, and a pretty song: "several plaintive whistled notes followed by a husky trilled whistle," as Marler described it. It is also a relatively tame bird, particularly conspicuous when it sings, repeating five or six songs per minute, often for long periods from the same perch. Taxonomists have identified five subspecies, one of which, *Zonotrichia leucophrys nuttalli,* is found only along the coast of California, generally in the chaparral, but also in and around city gardens. It was *nut-*

talli that Marler found outside his office on the Berkeley campus. Marler knew from the literature that the white-crowned sparrow had a system of song dialects throughout California, and though he spent his first two years at Berkeley recording several California and Mexican songbirds as he looked for a good subject for his research, by 1959 he had settled on the white-crown. For the next nine years he raised dozens of baby white-crowns in the laboratory and conducted a series of experiments with the birds. His work was modeled on Thorpe's, but it went beyond what Thorpe had done with the chaffinch.

During the breeding seasons of 1959 and 1960, Marler and a graduate student recorded white-crowned sparrows in three different locations: in the environs of Berkeley; at nearby Inspiration Point, two miles northeast of the city; and at Sunset Beach State Park, roughly one hundred miles south of Berkeley. Although it was well-known that the white-crowned sparrow had dialects, Marler began by carefully documenting this in the three different populations. In his study he divided the white-crown's song into two parts, its initial whistle and the trill that follows it. As he listened to the birds and examined the first sonograms he made, he decided that differences in the trill were the best index of the different dialects. The birds at Sunset Beach had three notes in each syllable of the trill, while the Berkeley birds usually had only one or two. The songs of the birds at Inspiration Point were similar to those of the Berkeley birds, though there were distinct differences, such as a syllable in the final trill with a more elaborate structure. If Marler had handed someone three dozen sonograms in random order from the three populations and instructed him to place them in three categories, it would not have been difficult. In 1962 Marler published a paper that summarized his findings. One of the differences between the white-crowned sparrow and the chaffinch was the former's lack of a song repertoire. While a chaffinch would sing up to six different songs, white-crowned sparrows sang only one. This played to Marler's advantage. It was easier to compare the songs of different populations when only one song was involved. The geographic variation occurred on a remarkably small scale as well. The birds at Inspiration Point were only two miles away from the Berkeley birds, yet they sang a different song.

What most caught Marler's attention, however, was evidence that suggested the white-crown learned its song in the first few weeks of its life. This simple observation led to an idea that was so thrilling in its potential ramifications it set off a sometimes hotly contested debate still in the air nearly half a century later. Near the end of the paper, Marler stated the tantalizing idea most on his mind: "In the white-crowned sparrow most of the learning seems to take place in the first few weeks of life while they are still in the locality of their birth. The stereotypy and stability of the song 'dialects' suggest that little exchange of individuals between populations occurs after the song patterns have been learned. Thus in this case there may be a potential relationship between song 'dialects' and the genetic constitution of populations, either indirect, if young birds simply do not wander far, or direct, if they wander but are attracted to breed in areas where they hear the song type which they learned in their youth." In other words, if, as preliminary evidence showed, the white-crowns learned their songs before they dispersed from their birth areas, then the birds were not dispersing beyond the area of the dialect they learned. Marler had already shown that in each population all the birds sang the same dialect. If the white-crowns were dispersing, they would be carrying their birth area dialect with them into a new population, creating a mixture of dialects. Thus, there appeared to be no gene flow across dialect boundaries, and the birds were, in effect, trapped on vocal desert islands—breeding only with each other. Since dialects were associated with songbirds and song-learning, this might explain why songbirds are the most diverse and numerous group of birds on the planet. Perhaps dialects isolated different populations of a species as surely as the islands of the Galápagos archipelago isolated Darwin's finches, resulting over time in the creation of new species.

Numerous leaps are being made here across some deep chasms, but this is generally Marler's line of thinking. And it is what made the observations so exciting. Marler was cautious, noting that much work remained before one could assert that dialects may have played a role in speciation in songbirds, but he quickly set out to add evidence that supported his interpretation. He needed to show convincingly that the white-crowns did indeed learn only before they left their birth area. In the next seven years Marler continued raising white-crowned sparrows, expanding his experiments in part to shed more light on the relationship between dialects and speciation. In one experiment, he captured two fledgling male white-crowns that he estimated were thirty-five days old, placed them in isolation from other sounds, but allowed them to see and hear one another, then waited to see how their songs would sound the following spring. The two birds sang completely normal white-crowned sparrow songs, suggesting that they had learned their songs from adults in the wild during the thirty-five days prior to their capture. Marler followed this experiment by taking two five-day-old birds from the nest and raising them in isolation. Each began singing at eight months of age, but developed abnormal songs. In another experiment he took one bird from the nest at three days old, put it in complete isolation, and played it recordings of white-crowned sparrow songs from days three to eight, then stopped and kept the bird isolated from sound until the following spring. At that point, it sang an abnormal song. Marler was slowly zeroing in on the precise period when the white-crown learned its song. It didn't learn before eight days old, but could learn all it needed to know before it was thirty-five days old. Next, Marler captured a group of birds between the ages of thirty and one hundred days, isolated them individually, and played recorded songs to them at various ages over the following months. All of the birds developed normal songs. He followed this with a more complicated experiment. Four nestlings brought into the laboratory between the ages of five and nine days (before they could learn) were isolated individually and exposed to white-crown songs at different ages, from days eight to twenty-eight for one bird, days thirty-five to fifty-six for another bird, and days fifty to seventy-one for the final two. He also exposed the birds to songs from two other species, Harris's sparrow, a bird with a song similar to the white-crown song but not a species that white-crowns come into contact with in the wild, and the song sparrow, whose song white-crowns would hear naturally in their shared habitat. The first two birds (trained days 8–28 and days 35–56) developed normal songs and displayed no effect from hearing the songs of the other species. The two birds whose training didn't begin until day fifty did not copy any of the songs they heard, including their own species song. This seemed to indicate convincingly that the white-crowned sparrow learned its song between eight and fifty days old, and not after that. Marler did one more experiment, exposing three birds taken from the nest to only song sparrow songs. These birds ignored the song sparrow songs and sang white-crown songs, though abnormal ones, never having heard the proper song during their song-learning period.

The paper Marler published made a seemingly open-and-shut case that the white-crowned sparrow learns its song during a relatively brief, critical period that lasts until it is approximately fifty days old. Then it stops learning. Furthermore, Marler demonstrated that the white-crown "learns selectively," which is to say that it ignores other species' songs in favor of its own. In addition, two of his students conducted playback experiments in the field with white-crowned sparrows that demonstrated that the birds responded more strongly to their own dialect than to others. Marler summarized his most significant conclusion: "Thus it begins to look as though one result of song-learning is an increase in the likelihood that male and female white-crowned sparrows will settle in the area where they were born. This might lead to a minor degree of inbreeding in local populations, perhaps permitting the evolution of physiological adaptations to local conditions." Again, Marler is cautious, saying "this *might* lead" and "*perhaps* permitting the evolution," but his experiments were carefully designed, his work meticulous in its attention to detail (when Marler momentarily opened the birds' cages for feeding or cleaning, he played "white noise" to lessen the chance of the birds hearing another bird), and his reasoning sound. Word spread quickly. Marler, still a young man, was becoming a major figure in ornithology. His work had already attracted high-caliber students who would soon spread his ideas and methods across the country as they took up teaching and research posts at prestigious institutions.

In 1966 when Marler was nearing the end of his nine-year study of the white-crowned sparrow, Don Kroodsma was majoring in chemistry at Hope College, a small school in Holland, Michigan, affiliated with the Dutch Reformed Church. The middle child of three boys, Kroodsma grew up in a quiet farming community a few miles east of Holland. Kroodsma's father, who worked at the gas station owned by the farmers' co-op, took his sons hunting and fishing and passed on to them a love of the outdoors. Kroodsma's older brother, Roger, was particularly interested in birds, and Kroodsma tagged along with him on bird outings. In college, Kroodsma enjoyed chemistry, but in the last semester of his junior year he decided he would take on a second major. In his senior year, with an intensity that would come to typify Kroodsma's career, he packed in all the courses he needed for a biology major. In his last semester he had to have a subject for a research project for a course in vertebrate biology and decided to study the birds in a nearby marsh. "I can still remember seeing a marsh wren, the first bird in my study, pop up to perch on a cattail. It was May 5, 1968," Kroodsma has written. "His tail was cocked over his head as he bobbed and swayed, buzzing and chattering, gurgling nonstop with what seemed like an endless variety of sounds."

Kroodsma decided that ornithology was his calling. He had already applied to several graduate schools, but now he realized he didn't know enough about birds. So, in the summer of 1968 after graduation from Hope College, he took two ornithology courses at the University of Michigan field station in Pellston. The courses were taught by one of the most well-known ornithologists of his generation, O. S. Pettingill. Sewall Pettingill also happened to be director of the Laboratory of Ornithology at Cornell, and he had brought with him a Nagra tape recorder. Kroodsma received financial aid for the courses that required him to do some kind of work while he was there. "Pettingill handed me the tape recorder and said, 'Record some bird songs for the Library of Natural Sounds and we'll be even.' He gave me a quick lesson in how to use the recorder and then told me to go out and get some bird sounds. It was as if he knew where I was headed."

A few days after the course ended, Kroodsma married his college sweetheart, got in a car, and honeymooned across the United States on his way to Oregon State University. When he arrived in Corvallis, Oregon, in the fall of 1968, he wasn't certain what area of ornithology he would take up. He knew little about the biology department or its reputation, but soon discovered an ornithologist, John Wiens, who was doing field studies on the flocking dynamics of grassland birds. Wiens would have been happy to have his new student join him in his work with grassland birds, but Kroodsma set out to find something that would be his alone. "I had been given a nice financial package," Kroodsma says, "which included a state car I could use. I drove everywhere looking for a project. I went into the rain forest of the coastal mountain range and on to the Pacific coast, then back across Willamette Valley to the east and into the Cascade mountains and out the other side into the central Oregon desert. I'd get out of the car and look around and listen for birds. I was just hoping a dissertation subject would jump out at me."

The fall semester went by, and Kroodsma still had no idea what to focus on for his Ph.D. In his second semester he took a behavioral biology course from Wiens that demanded a research project. For several days he cast about for an idea. Then one morning he looked out the window of his basement apartment and noticed a Bewick's wren singing in the trees in his neighbor's garden. There had been a light snowfall the night before, but now the sun was out and the wren sang exuberantly. Behind him, across the valley, Kroodsma could see the snowcapped peaks of the Cascade mountains, but the tiny wren held his attention. With each song, the bird tilted his head back and poured out a complex series of notes. Kroodsma, stepping outdoors, stood and listened. Suddenly, the wren switched to a different song. He sang for several minutes, then switched to another song. How many songs did he have? In the biology department, Kroodsma had discovered a tape recorder and sonograph sitting on a shelf, and now he quickly put them to use. Over the next few days, he recorded and graphed the wren's songs. Each evening, he watched the bird slip up under the eaves of his neighbor's shed to roost. The next morning, Kroodsma was up early to listen to him again. Eventually, he counted sixteen different songs. And he noted that the wren sang forty to fifty repetitions of one song before switching to the next.

Kroodsma had his project, and it became the beginning of his life's work. He started reading everything he could find on birdsong. By 1969, Peter Marler had published several papers on birdsong, including his first report on white-crowned sparrows, and Robert Hinde, who had been director of the Madingley Field Station when Marler worked there with Thorpe, had just published a book, *Bird Vocalizations: Their Relations to Current Problems in Biology and Psychology*. The study of birdsong was taking shape as a discipline, and the issues related to it still being defined. Kroodsma was interested in Marler's ideas about how young birds learned their songs. Based on the few studies that had been done, Marler seemed to believe that most species learned from their fathers and neighbors in the first few months of their lives.

"I started asking questions about my Bewick's wren," Kroodsma says. "What is his neighbor doing? How about the Bewick's wrens a few miles away?" Kroodsma recorded more wrens nearby, then drove to Finley National Wildlife Refuge ten miles away and recorded there. He compared the songs. There were different dialects. Kroodsma reread Marler's paper on the white-crowned sparrow. The results of Marler's lab experiments appeared undeniable: young white-crowns learned from their fathers, or other adults in their birth area. But Kroodsma wasn't so sure: "That was the point at which I said to myself, 'Well, it's pretty shaky relying on the confines of the laboratory to make those inferences. Playing songs to birds over loudspeakers is highly artificial.'"

In those same weeks, Kroodsma came across a paper on wren-tits in California that showed it was possible to band baby birds and relocate some of them if the birds didn't travel too far away. Because Bewick's wrens did not migrate, he guessed that they usually stayed within a mile or two of where they were born. If he tape-recorded baby wrens in their birth area and again after they moved away, he might be able to learn from whom the birds learned their songs rather than rely on laboratory experiments. John Wiens cautioned Kroodsma that he shouldn't gamble his Ph.D. dissertation on this. Capturing baby wrens and banding them was challenging enough, but finding them a year later was risky. Kroodsma, though, could not be dissuaded. "You've heard the phrase *stubborn Dutchman*? That was me," he says.

In the spring of 1969 Kroodsma set out to prove he could understand something about song-learning through field-work. He also had a hunch—despite conventional wisdom to the contrary—that the young wrens were learning songs from adults they settled next to after leaving their birth area. As his study site, he chose nearby Finley National Wildlife Refuge, where the wrens were plentiful. Finley National Wildlife Refuge begins on the west side of the Willamette Valley and extends into the rolling hills that are the first uplift of the coastal mountains. Sections of the refuge are woodlands, dominated by Oregon oak and ash with a dense understory of blackberry, snowberry, and nutka rose, the latter providing the kind of thick cover favored by wrens. Other parts of the refuge are nearly indistinguishable from the agricultural land of the valley and, in fact, are planted with grain to sustain Canada geese during migration. In these open areas only old fencerows, which are overgrown with brambles and shrubs, are good wren habitat, as are the briar patches and thickets that have formed along the creek there. In the spring and summer of 1969 and 1970, Kroodsma walked through the refuge listening for wrens, familiarizing himself with their habits and paying attention to how the birds divided up the refuge into territories. Kroodsma mapped out a study site that was roughly four thousand acres, approximately 80 percent of the refuge. As a result, he had a grid 1.5 miles east-west by 4.5 miles north-south. When he drew in the wren territories, he had what looked like a half-completed jigsaw puzzle, each piece representing a wren territory, the blank spots reflecting areas without wrens. On this page he would write the numbers of the adult male wrens that he banded, placing them like pins on a map.

Wrens are small, quick, brazen birds, and though they are not particularly strong fliers—their short, rounded wings don't give them much power—they are active, flitting rapidly through the underbrush, popping into the open now and then to survey their world, then diving back into the thick ground cover where their streaked and spotted brown or brown-gray bodies make them difficult for predators to see. They are also among the most vocal of birds (they are closely related to the mockingbird), and their songs, full of buzzes and warbles and gurgles, are often complicated and varied, sometimes musical, sometimes simply noisy. The song of the Bewick's wren is one of the prettiest of North American wrens', admired by America's earliest naturalists. "The song is sweet and exquisitely tender—one of the sweetest and tenderest strains that I know. It recalls that of the song sparrow, but is more prolonged, varied, and expressive," wrote one naturalist. A typical song begins with a raspy phrase, then dips in pitch to a warbled note, followed by a short whistle, and finally a strong, clear trill that ends abruptly, all of it lasting about two seconds.

The Bewick's wren, one of ten species of wrens found in North America, is relatively common in much of the West, and most important to Kroodsma's study, in this part of Oregon it remains on its territory year-round. They begin singing in earnest by March. By April they are breeding, and by late May the first young birds, two weeks old, begin to leave the nest. The young wrens remain with the father and mother for two to three weeks as they test their wings and learn to forage, then set out on their own. Some may stay near the territory where they were born. Others will relocate, moving through adjacent territories until they find a place for themselves, often not moving more than two or three territories away. By August the males of these newly fledged wrens will already look to establish their own territory, often slipping into the edge of an adult male's property just at the time the adult's hormones are waning, the breeding season behind him.

In the spring of 1970, Kroodsma's plan was to capture and band adult wrens and chart their territories. A few weeks later he would capture baby wrens still with their parents. He would then know the family history of many of the Bewick's wrens in the area. If all went well, he would be able to relocate some of the young wrens the following spring and make note whether they were near their father's territory and singing the dialect of that area or were in a new territory and were either still singing their father's dialect or the dialect of their new area.

Kroodsma got up each day well before first light and drove to Finley with a mist net, his tape recorder, and two small speakers. The key to capturing a wren was to find an open area in the bird's territory where one could set up the net, then figure out if this area was a natural flyway. "The fun part was to think like a wren," Kroodsma says. "They would go from one dense bush to another, so I'd look for a pathway between them. If there was vegetation that was too high on one side of the net, they'd fly over the net, so it had to be just the right spot, for example a small opening between two rosebushes near the center of his territory."

Once the mist net was in place, Kroodsma would place a small speaker about five yards to one side of the base of the net, then run a cable from the speaker to the tape recorder that he would operate from a short distance away, out of sight. Kroodsma hoped for cloudy, windless days. The darker the sky the less visible the black netting would be. The calmer the air the less the net would move. On a good day Kroodsma could go into a territory, set the net up, and capture and band a bird in half an hour. Now and then if he guessed wrong when he set the net up, the bird flew parallel to it, going back and forth along the net looking for the intruder he could hear singing. In such cases Kroodsma set up a second speaker a few yards off to the other side of the net, played a song or two, then a song from the speaker on the other side, which pulled the bird this way, then that way, like a puppet, sending it directly into the net. If the lay of the land and the vegetation encouraged the bird to fly high over the net, Kroodsma had a solution. He would have something in his hand, perhaps a stone, to throw into the air above the flying bird. The bird would swoop down to avoid the object and run into the net.

By the end of spring, including his work from the previous year, Kroodsma had banded more than three hundred adult male wrens. The next step was to band their offspring. Kroodsma would have been happy if he could have banded the baby wrens before they left the nest. In fact, he tried to band nestlings, but without much success. The Bewick's wren, like many wrens, prefers to nest in cavities, the more inaccessible to mammals the better (and hence the family name, Troglodytidae, from the Greek *trogle* and *dy[ein]*—one who creeps into holes, a "cave dweller"). When the birds nested, Kroodsma watched when he saw parent birds diving into the brush, then he followed, sometimes on hands and knees through the brambles. In the end, though, he had managed to find only a few nests, banding seventeen nestlings.

Now, he faced capturing the recently fledged birds, for which his playback trick would be useless. The birds were too young to respond to a rival's song, real or fake. Kroodsma walked the refuge listening and watching for family groups. When he came across a group, he set the net up, then circled back behind the birds and tried to herd them toward it. The young birds, only a day or two out of the nest, followed the parents closely. If the territory included a fencerow of brambles, it was easier. He could herd the birds down the fencerow and into the net, which he'd set up at a gap in the dense cover. If the net was positioned just right in the opening, he would have a net full of birds. Day after day he went to the refuge before dawn and chased wren families toward his mist net. At the end of the summer of 1970, he had captured and banded ninety-seven baby wrens. At fledgling age, male and female Bewick's wrens are indistinguishable, so Kroodsma used the general principle that applied to avian hatchlings: half of the ninety-seven should be male birds. That left him with forty-nine birds for his study. He would have six months to wonder how many would survive the winter, and of those that survived, how many would remain in his study site.

The next March, Kroodsma was back at the refuge patrolling the wren territories and looking for banded birds. The adult male birds he had banded the previous year were still defending the same territories, if they'd survived the winter. The baby wrens, now in their first year as adult birds, were defending their own territories. As he walked the grid, he made notes, confirming the location of the adult males from the previous year. On March 9 he was walking through the bottomland along the creek, noting that most of the males were in the same place they had been the year before, although some were unbanded and thus of unknown origin. As he moved along, checking off each male in his notebook, he came across a bird with a new band combination. The bird had an aluminum band on the left leg, and the bands on his right leg were green above red. He checked his notebook with the list of banded birds. Here was what he was waiting for: a bird he'd banded last year as a fledgling.

His notebook indicated that he'd banded the bird when it was just over two weeks old on June 19 the previous summer. It was one of three nestlings from a family he'd herded into a net. They were numbers 324, 325, and 326. This was 326. He was born a half mile to the north. Writing about it later, Kroodsma traced in his imagination the bird's journey over the past months: "During early July, when only four or five weeks old, he left home in search of his own territory. He undoubtedly wandered some, searching for a home of his own over several weeks, but by early August he was most likely already here, perhaps carving out a small territory in the thicket of blackberries and roses where I now stood. I had found lots of other young birds fighting for their territories last

August, but somehow overlooked 326. Had I been here last August, I would have heard his jingly beginnings. Unlike an adult male, who sings a 2-second song and then pauses for 5 or 6 seconds, this youngster would have babbled continuously, sometimes for 10 to 20 seconds, mixing his innate *see* call with snippets of songs that he had learned from adult wrens during his travels. He started learning his songs while still with his father, who often sang just before feeding him. En route to this eventual location, he heard still other males; and then, here, as he established a foothold in the tangles, the resident adults harassed him, singing their 'go away' threats in his face, giving him ample opportunity to memorize the local songs. In the face of such threats, he would retire to the dense underbrush, where he would softly babble, never singing loudly out in the open like an adult. Through September, October, and into November he sang, gradually improving his efforts; he sang little during the rainy winter, but then revved up again early in the new year, until I found him here."

On the morning of March 9 it was cold, in the forties, still predawn, and 326 sang without enthusiasm. The Oregon ash and oak trees were leafless, and the wrens stayed close to the thickets of nutka rose and blackberry bushes. Kroodsma recorded his songs, then turned his attention to recording the neighboring wrens. The males to the east, west, and north were each on the same territory as the previous year. Kroodsma recorded until he had good samples for each of the birds. The following morning, Kroodsma returned to the territory, where he found 326 again in the same spot. In the minutes before dawn, the male to the west sang first, but then 326 appeared at the top of an ash tree and began singing. Kroodsma recorded for four hours. He had his first example, but he needed more. In the days that followed, he walked through the refuge, skipping more quickly through the areas where he had confirmed banded birds, and looking closely at every bird he didn't know. Adult males from the previous year hadn't all survived, and it was critical that Kroodsma not only relocate some of the banded babies, but also find them on territories next to known, banded birds. By the end of the summer, he had relocated six of the male wrens that he had banded as fledgling birds the year before, a good percentage given all the factors working against him. Only one of those six birds had remained near his father. The other five had dispersed into new territories; 326 was in an ideal situation—three of his immediate neighbors were banded.

In the fall and winter that followed, Kroodsma spent weeks producing sonograms of the songs he had recorded. He needed to make dozens of sonograms for each of the five males to make certain that he had samples of all of the songs that each bird sang, then dozens more sonograms for the other birds he had recorded, hundreds of sonograms overall. In 1971, before the days of personal computers, producing sonograms was a slow process. Each sonogram was produced on a six-by-fourteen-inch sheet of paper that Kroodsma wrapped around the metal drum of the machine. As the drum turned, a spark jumped between a metal stylus and the metal drum, burning an image in the thermal-sensitive paper, and sending up little clouds of smoke and the distinctive smell of ozone. Fortunately, the wren's song lasted only about two seconds, because the sonogram was capable of recording just 2.4 seconds of sound on one sheet of paper. Kroodsma stacked up the pages as he worked. When he had all the sonograms, he set out to compare the songs of sons with their fathers and their new neighbors. With the case of bird 326, his father, and three neighbors, he had five stacks of sonograms. Kroodsma felt certain the young birds were learning new songs from their neighbors and essentially abandoning their father's songs, and since he expected the sonograms to reveal this, he guarded against his own bias by coding the sheets of paper for the father and three neighbors so he wouldn't know which sonogram belonged to which bird. He wanted to make sure that he didn't just see what he wanted to see.

He took one of the songs of bird 326 and laid it out on the table. He then shuffled through the other sonograms looking for a distinctive note that appeared similar in all the sonograms. The wren's song typically had four phrases. The first phrase might look like a cartoonish eyebrow on the page; the second phrase was a series of thin hash marks that represented a brief, rapid trill; the third phrase was usually a thick splotch, the clear whistled note; and then came the second series of hash marks for the final trill, the repeated note of the trill so even that it looked like a rapid heartbeat on a monitor. In this brief two-second song, the various notes went up and down in pitch from 2.5 kilohertz to 8 kilohertz. Kroodsma pored over them as a handwriting analyst would stare at the loops and squiggles and flourishes of writing samples.

When Kroodsma was finished grouping the songs of 326 and his father and neighbors by similarities, he went to his notebook and pulled out his code. Slowly he began to see that bird 326 and his immediate neighbors shared songs that 326 did not share with his father. In one song, the father's final trill was significantly shorter than the trill of 326 and the three neighbors. In another, the father's trill was slower. It was exactly what Kroodsma had hoped for. When he was done with his comparisons, wren 326 clearly shared more songs with his immediate neighbors than he did with his father, whom he had left behind. His songs were almost identical to those of 229, his neighbor to the west, and next closest to 221 to the east, then to 223 to the north. He shared a few songs with his father, 94, as well, a kilometer to the north, but "when it matters, when the songs of his new neighborhood differ from those of the father, the yearling always rejects his father's variant and sings the local songs. Just once I caught him reverting to a peculiar phrase sung only by his father. Clearly he had learned his father's songs during the first four or five weeks of his life, but once he left home, he was eager to replace Dad's songs with songs that would match those of males who would be his neighbors for the rest of his life." The situations of the other five birds were not as ideal as that of 326. The important thing was that Kroodsma knew the fathers of the other five, even if he wasn't certain of the identity of all of the neighbors. The same pattern prevailed. The birds shared more songs with their immediate neighbors than they did with their fathers. Kroodsma's stubbornness had paid off. He had proof that not all songbirds learned from their fathers or others in their birth area as was commonly thought.

More than thirty years later, Kroodsma still thinks of the Bewick's wren study as some of his best work, and he remembers the great pleasure of discovering that his instincts were right. It proved to him that fieldwork was necessary to understand singing behavior. It did not, however, have any immediate impact on the greater world of avian bioacoustics. Despite Kroodsma's study, the prevailing wisdom that songbirds learned from their fathers or birth-area neighbors did not begin to change for some time. Laboratory work, which could control all the variables, carried with it the aura of certainty. Fieldwork was replete with problematic conditions and variables. Kroodsma's research went into his dissertation, which was added to the stacks at the Oregon State University library, the work of a young student not long off the farm. Kroodsma recalls that Marler's laboratory work on white-crowned sparrows was so convincing that when Kroodsma met Luis Baptista, another young birdsong enthusiast, in the spring of 1971, Baptista told Kroodsma of a house finch he recorded in the field that was singing the song of a white-crowned sparrow. Baptista's explanation was that the finch had surely been raised by white-crowned sparrows when its mother somehow deposited an egg in the wrong nest. This was more far-fetched, though not unheard of, than the simpler explanation that the finch had picked up the song later on, a notion, of course, that contradicted findings of lab experiments.

That same year Kroodsma had a talk with Jerry Verner, a former postdoctoral student of Marler's, who had gone on to teach at Central Washington University. Verner had given a seminar at Oregon State on the singing behavior of marsh wrens that had inspired Kroodsma, so Kroodsma sought him out at the annual conference of the American Ornithologists' Union in Seattle in 1971. Marler had published a major paper, supported by dozens of studies over the previous decade, that neatly laid out what was then known about birds learning their songs from their fathers or birth-area neighbors. It was solid, careful work, and Marler was the founder of avian bio-acoustics in the United States. Many of the growing number of ornithologists interested in the field were former students of Marler's. Still, as he talked with Verner, Kroodsma expressed his misgivings about the conventional wisdom, and about drawing conclusions from laboratory work. "I was explaining this to Jerry," Kroodsma recalls, "and he said something like, 'Well, go do something about it.'"

Kroodsma did. He applied to work with Marler on a post-doctoral fellowship. If he had doubts about what could be learned about songbirds from laboratory experiments, it would be good for him to learn the theoretical nuances and practical considerations of such work, and learn it from the master.

In the fall of 1972, Kroodsma moved cross-country to Millbrook, New York. Rockefeller University, which had lured Marler away from Berkeley, had established a new field station for avian bioacoustics on the grounds of a former country estate. "I was scared to death," Kroodsma says, "a small-town boy in a big Eastern establishment. I had kind of hustled through graduate school in a somewhat out-of-the-way place and had not really met that many people. I didn't feel I could hold my own in that kind of company. It was a sink-or-swim environment." Marler was attracting students and colleagues from all over North America, and avian bioacoustics was growing rapidly. Marler immediately invited Kroodsma to join him in a study of the factors that influenced young red-winged blackbirds to learn their song. He had discovered in the laboratory the blackbirds were just as likely to learn the song of an oriole as their own song. The study failed to produce useful data, so Kroodsma took up another project Marler had in mind, but this too came to a dead end. Marler suggested Kroodsma do a comparative study of song-learning in two closely related species, for which Kroodsma chose song sparrows and swamp sparrows. Though this produced interesting results, and a publication, Kroodsma lost interest.

During that first year, Kroodsma discovered Marler was

willing to let him follow his interests, and after those initial aborted efforts, Kroodsma took full advantage. Young biologists often stick with a subject when they find that it yields results, building on it year by year and publication by publication, a safe way to establish a career. But Kroodsma was restless. He moved from one species to another, from laboratory work to fieldwork, from raising birds in soundproof chambers to banding babies in the field. He studied the effects of large song repertoires in song sparrows; counted the number of songs a single brown thrasher had in his repertoire (an astounding two thousand songs, one of the most frequently cited facts in bioacoustics); analyzed the amazing ten-second-long song of the winter wren, the "pinnacle of complexity," Kroodsma called it; conducted a carefully controlled laboratory experiment that pinpointed the sensitive period for song-learning in the marsh wren; and performed a series of tests with canaries that established that female canaries nested faster and laid more eggs when exposed to males with larger song repertoires.

Although Kroodsma did not settle on one line of research, he became increasingly aware of what it would take to build a successful career. He was surrounded by some of the best young scientists in the country, and Marler set high standards. Kroodsma remembers the seminars Marler held. "An invited guest would present his research, and at the end of the presentation, Marler had this way of starting out with a self-deprecating, humble comment, something like 'Oh, well, I don't really know much about this field,' and then you just knew what was coming. He'd absolutely skewer the poor guy on the weakest point of the study." Marler provided a great opportunity for his postdoc fellows so he expected them to be completely dedicated to their work. On summer days after lunch, many of the postdocs would play volleyball on the lawn, and when the matches ran long, Marler would come out of his office and stand and stare until he'd made it clear that lunch hour was over. Rivalries developed, and Marler himself was involved in more than one uncomfortable disagreement with colleagues whose work contradicted his. Kroodsma remembers one of the other postdocs talking about these rivalries and the single-minded devotion Marler had to his research. "If this is what you have to do to be successful, I don't want any part of it," he said to Kroodsma.

In contrast, Rockefeller brought out Kroodsma's competitive nature. "I played the game intensely," he once told me. "It was a huge juggling act, and sometimes work overshadowed family, and families left. I was lucky to have a tolerant wife." Kroodsma worked hard to make a name for himself by publishing papers where they would be noticed. Scientists often talk about "top-tier" or "premier" journals—those publications that regularly feature the best and most important papers in their field. For ornithology, *The Auk* is generally considered to be the most prestigious journal, followed by *The Condor, The Wilson Bulletin,* and the *Journal of Field Ornithology.* Young ornithologists typically begin publishing in lesser journals. Often they coauthor papers with their adviser, getting credit only as "second author." Many never publish in the top journals at all, and even further out of reach are *Science* and *Nature,* the two internationally famous journals that draw from the best in the sciences. ("As reported in *Nature*" is often the lead-in to stories on National Public Radio and television news.) In 1972, his first year at Rockefeller, Kroodsma published a paper in *The Auk* and a second one in *The Wilson Bulletin.* In 1973, he published again in *The Auk,* followed by two papers in *The Condor.* Then he set his sights higher. In the next four years he published twice in *Nature* and once in *Science.* He was sole author on all but a couple. One exception was his paper on the brown thrasher's repertoire of two thousand songs, for which Kroodsma had enlisted help in counting the songs. The second author listed is L. D. Parker, Kroodsma's mother-in-law.

If anything is more important to one's career than high-profile publications, it is how much grant money one raises to fund research. For scientists at major universities the rule is "no grant money, no tenure." The competition for grants awarded by the National Science Foundation is especially fierce, and arguably greater yet in fields like avian bioacoustics. Most NSF money goes for research in areas such as molecular biology, which may yield discoveries beneficial to human health and medicine. Kroodsma was awarded an NSF grant in his fourth year at Rockefeller, and this was followed by a string of NSF grants that funded his research without interruption for the next twenty-three years. His reputation grew accordingly. One year the National Science Foundation actually gave him 50 percent more money than he had asked for and extended the grant period from two years to three.

From Marler and the others at Millbrook, Kroodsma learned the details of laboratory experiments with birds kept in soundproof chambers, and he became proficient at raising baby birds by hand. But even as he conducted the laboratory experiments, he had doubts. For his study on the sensitive period during the song-learning phase of the marsh wren, he played a group of songs to young marsh wrens for three days, a different group of songs for six days, and yet another group for nine days. It was an elegantly simple experiment. The following spring he listened to the birds sing to determine which songs they had duplicated—an indication of when their sensitive learning period was at its height. The results appeared unequivocal. "That was one of my publications in *Nature*," Kroodsma told me recently, "and of course it was all done with loudspeakers in the laboratory. The graphs looked pretty clear-cut, and those who believe in the quality of laboratory studies and what you can learn there probably still think they're pretty neat, but I'm not sure what they tell us about what the bird is actually doing in the real world."

Kroodsma hadn't forgotten that his study of the Bewick's wren contradicted what seemed to be solid principles established by Marler's lab work with the white-crowned sparrow. During the next few years he saw other research unfold that also undermined Marler's initial laboratory results. Luis Baptista repeated Marler's experiments but used "live tutors"—living birds—to supply the songs the baby sparrows heard rather than songs played over loudspeakers. He discovered the young sparrows would continue learning songs beyond the fifty-day period Marler had established as the end of their learning period. "If I had done my fieldwork on white-crowned sparrows—the popular white rat of ornithology—I think the whole field could have taken a much earlier leap out of this laboratory dogma," Kroodsma says. "But what it took was Luis Baptista working on white-crowned sparrows. Then he did fieldwork to show essentially the same thing I had with the Bewick's wren." About the same time, Gerhard Thielche in Germany was discovering that he couldn't get young woodcreepers to learn songs from loudspeakers at all, but that they learned fine from live adult males. Studies with zebra finches were revealing similar distinctions between learning from loudspeakers compared to live birds. Kroodsma himself conducted an experiment with marsh wrens that showed young birds would learn songs at a much later date from live tutors than they would from songs played over loudspeakers.

Kroodsma's distrust of conclusions drawn from laboratory experiments would grow firmer over the years. It wasn't that lab work was useless and fieldwork essential, but that much of the avian bioacoustics establishment placed too much faith in the former. Lab experiments seemed to provide clear-cut results because researchers could control the variables. In a song-learning study, for instance, one could keep birds out of sight from each other and expose them to songs, thus assuring—it seemed—that they were responding only to auditory stimuli. In other words, if a bird reacted a certain way to songs played to him, it was because of the songs and nothing else, whereas it would be impossible to know if birds in the wild were responding to songs or visual displays by another bird, a combination of both, or some other stimulus since all of those elements were present in the wild. Lab work could be vitally important, Kroodsma believed, but only if researchers understood its limits. It was possible, for instance, to manipulate out important variables, as Marler had done with the white-crowned sparrow when he used songs played on loudspeakers. Baptista's experiments showed that some social component—an interaction between young and adult birds, present when he used a live tutor—was important in song-learning, a component that the controls of Marler's experiment had eliminated.

Today, many still consider fieldwork "difficult, dull and somewhat old-fashioned" as Clive Catchpole and P. J. B. Slater put it in their book, *Bird Song: Biological Themes and Variations*. Michael Beecher, a friend of Kroodsma's, devoted a book chapter to the issue, noting that "studies in natural populations in the field have always been shunned in favor of laboratory experiments." Beecher is acutely aware of the problems with lab experiments because the results of his own studies with hand-raised song sparrows were later contradicted by fieldwork he did. In the lab Beecher found that young birds that learned their songs by listening to several different adult song sparrows picked elements from each of the different adult songs and created their own unique songs, hybrids essentially of the various adult songs. Later, working with banded birds, he learned that young song sparrows in the wild did something radically different—they copied specific songs from their neighbors completely and precisely. Beecher went on to describe several other laboratory results that were misleading. Fieldwork is essential, Beecher concludes, and it should precede laboratory work. One should know something of a bird's singing behavior in the wild and environmental and social factors that might influence it before conducting lab experiments. How else would one know appropriate questions to ask in a controlled experiment? Kroodsma has noted that hundreds of laboratory studies have been conducted on song-learning in zebra finches—a bird that is easily raised in captivity—but that we know little about how zebra finches act in the wild. Kroodsma summarized his feelings in a 1991 paper: "To experiment first is human, to describe first, divine."

Of all the work Kroodsma did at Rockefeller, it was a failed study that led him to the most absorbing work of his early career. Less than a year after Kroodsma arrived at Rockefeller, he began thinking about marsh wrens. He remembered a seminar on the marsh wren that Jerry Verner had given at Oregon State a couple of years earlier, and he was fascinated with Verner's discoveries. Many songbirds with a repertoire of songs sing one several times before going on to the next, but the marsh wrens that Verner had studied raced through their entire repertoire, singing over a hundred different songs in seven minutes. When Verner taped the songs of one male and then played them on a loudspeaker to males in the neighborhood, the bird's neighbor not only matched the rival song for song, but sometimes skipped ahead in the sequence. If the sequence of songs was A,B,C,D,E,F, and so forth, the neighboring wren would respond to song A by either matching it with his own rendition of song A, or skipping ahead to song B. What could account for a rivalry so intense that it produced this remarkable ritualistic display of one-upmanship?

Like the Bewick's wrens Kroodsma had studied in Oregon, the western marsh wrens were resident birds. Because they remained on territories year-round, the male birds got to know their neighbors well. What's more, marsh wrens are polygynous. Verner discovered that the males he was studying mated with as many as three or four females, leaving several bachelor wrens around him ("evolutionary losers," Kroodsma calls them). The male marsh wren, despite having several nests with his young in them, acted as a parent to only one brood. Verner wondered why a female would mate with a male that wouldn't help her raise the young. What advantage could there be in that? What he discovered was that the dominant males that mated with several females owned the best real estate, a territory that was, say, particularly rich in insect life. Thus, the female was better off on her own in this good territory than she was getting help from a male in a poorer territory. Furthermore, the marsh wrens had exceptionally small territories, substantially smaller than those of other wren species and other songbirds in general. They were crammed in like city dwellers. The debate over property rights was intense. This fierce competition in such proximity had apparently developed into the ritualistic countersinging, not to mention occasional outbreaks of violence when the wrens would destroy each other's eggs.

Kroodsma kept in touch with Verner, by now a good friend, and in 1974 when Verner took a job in Illinois, he and Kroodsma decided to work together on sedge wrens and marsh wrens, which coexisted in the marshes and wet prairies of Illinois. Kroodsma and Verner recorded two male marsh wrens extensively in June of 1974, but when Kroodsma analyzed the recordings, he was disappointed to find the birds had on average only thirty songs, far fewer than the average of more than a hundred that Verner had found in the marsh wrens in central Washington. Kroodsma thought this might be an anomaly. But wrens were in his blood now, and the following summer he set up an elaborate project with marsh wrens along the Hudson River, near Rockefeller. His plan was to build on what Verner had already learned about counter-singing in marsh wrens. During the summer of 1975 Kroodsma and five colleagues from Rockefeller went to a marsh along the Hudson River once a week and taped a group of neighboring marsh wrens. They used several recorders that were synchronized so that Kroodsma would have on tape the songs of birds in a group singing back and forth to each other. With such a collection of songs, he could analyze exactly how the countersinging occurred. Again, Kroodsma was disappointed. The birds didn't countersing as he'd expected. And these birds too sang fewer songs, forty to sixty, than the marsh wrens Verner recorded in the West. Kroodsma's ambitious project came to a halt. He put the tapes in a box and set it aside.

A few years later, in 1979, he returned to the marsh wren to investigate the disparity between the repertoires of the Eastern and Western birds. Kroodsma collected baby marsh wrens in the West and also babies from the East, raised them, and then, working with two other Rockefeller ornithologists, compared the differences in the brains of the Western marsh wren and the Eastern marsh wren. The study revealed that the Western marsh wren devotes 50 percent more brain space to the overall task of singing. This was a remarkable difference, and it made the Eastern and Western marsh wrens look like two different species.

In 1980, the marsh wren puzzle still incomplete, Kroodsma's appointment at Rockefeller University ended, and he took a teaching position at the University of Massachusetts. He had spent eight years working under nearly ideal circumstances. He had been immersed in a kind of birdsong think tank, surrounded each day by others working on various aspects of avian bioacoustics. And he'd had few duties other than to conduct his own research. At the University of Massachusetts he had to teach and supervise the research of graduate students. Still, Kroodsma continued his research at his customary pace. He worked on willow and alder fly-catchers, phoebes, and prothonotary and blue-winged warblers. Then, in 1986, he returned to the marsh wren. He wanted to resolve the issue that had been on his mind since he'd discovered the Eastern birds had far fewer songs and didn't match each other's song when they countersang. He began to wonder if the marsh wrens in California and those in New York were in fact the same species. The difference in the singing behavior of marsh wrens might change gradually from east to west, and looking only at the differences between the birds was misleading. Song sparrows in Alaska are nearly twice the size of song sparrows in California, and they have darker plumage as well. But if one looks at song sparrows along a continuum from south to north, it becomes apparent that this change takes place gradually. In such a case, it's clear the bird is one species that varies in color and size. When the change occurs gradually along a geographical line, it's known as a *cline*. So if Eastern marsh wrens have fewer songs, but the number of songs slowly increases from one area to the next moving westward, then the marsh wren is most likely one species. An abrupt change would suggest that there were two species.

Kroodsma flew to Sioux Falls, South Dakota, to see how marsh wrens sing in the Great Plains, where some Eastern and Western species occur side by side. In a marsh outside of Sioux Falls he found plenty of marsh wrens, but all of them sounded like Eastern birds, so the next day he got in the car and drove west to Lake Andes National Wildlife Refuge. There, too, all the birds sang like Eastern marsh wrens. A day later he drove farther southwest, stopping at Swan Lake in Nebraska, where the marsh wrens sounded like Western birds. He had crossed the great marsh-wren divide, and the change was dramatic, not gradual. Kroodsma wasn't satisfied. He wanted to know what the birds east and west of this area sounded like, so over the next few days he visited other sites. To the west, with a few exceptions, he found wrens with Western songs; to the east, he came across Eastern marsh wren songs again. When he returned to the university and analyzed the songs he'd recorded, he felt more certain that the marsh wren was really two species. If he could locate a marsh where some birds were singing pure Eastern songs and others were singing pure Western songs, he would have even stronger evidence that the Eastern and Western wrens were breeding only with their own kind—a critical criterion for determining species status.

The following spring, on a tip from a friend, he flew to Saskatchewan and drove to the Qu'Appelle River Valley. His first stop was Last Mountain Lake, and there, side by side, were marsh wrens singing like Verner's Western birds and marsh wrens singing like the Eastern birds Kroodsma had recorded in New York. "That was a eureka moment," Kroodsma says. "The continent suddenly took shape for me." Over the next few years Kroodsma continued working on the wrens. He returned to the Qu'Appelle River Valley and recorded more birds, analyzed song repertoires, tabulated the results, and enlisted colleagues to analyze the DNA of the Western and Eastern birds. The results confirmed they were genetically different. Then, surprisingly, Kroodsma did something that foreshadowed the mixed feelings he would later develop about his chosen profession. His curiosity satisfied, he dropped the issue, never publishing the results. Today, the data from the study are stored in several boxes in his basement.

In 1986, when Kroodsma began working again on marsh wrens, he was forty years old—middle-aged and midcareer. He had a stellar reputation and had settled into a position with one of the top research universities in the East. He was, however, about to enter a season of turmoil. Although Kroodsma had participated fully in the build-your-career game, he was increasingly disturbed by the politics of his profession and by colleagues who put their careers above the integrity of their work. Some years earlier, he dropped his subscription to a major science journal and refused to submit his own work, despite the exposure and recognition it would receive. He'd heard too many stories of authors whose work had been rejected by the journal only to have it reconsidered and accepted when the authors argued with the editors. It wasn't necessarily that the papers weren't worthy. Kroodsma was just disgusted with the process by which they were accepted—as if, he said, papers were being selected according to the aggressiveness of their authors.

In the late 1980s, the Biology Department at the University of Massachusetts established a new program that combined neuroscience and animal behavior. Kroodsma became one of the faculty involved in building the program, but a couple of years later a new program director was hired who rubbed Kroodsma the wrong way. Kroodsma found him to be aggressive and rude. The director's appointment added to what was becoming an unpleasant environment in the department, which, like biology departments everywhere, was divided between the "skin-out" biologists and the "skin-in" biologists—those who studied whole animals versus those who worked on animal cells and molecules. The latter is where the money is. The big grants go to those whose work might have some direct application to human life. Biochemistry and neuroscience promise discoveries that can lead to patents and advances in medicine. Money is power in academia, of course, and the molecular biologists at the University of Massachusetts asserted their superiority.

Kroodsma resigned from the neuroscience and animal behavior program and was so disturbed he asked the university to transfer him to the Department of Forestry and Wildlife. The request was denied. The split between what Kroodsma calls "the cell smashers" and "the real people who are enthused about studying whole plants and animals" grew worse. A few years later at a department meeting one of the cell smashers said ecology wasn't worthy of being called a science or a discipline. There was no need to consider hiring new faculty to teach ecology because it was useless for students to take ecology courses, and in fact students shouldn't be required to take ecology at all. Kroodsma now refers to the occasion as Black Monday. He has not been back to a department meeting since.

On the phone one afternoon, he recalled how he had been hired at the University of Massachusetts. The university had advertised one position for a parasitologist and one for an ornithologist, but it was understood they would hire only one person—the strongest candidate regardless of field. Kroodsma was one of the two finalists. The members of the biology department were more interested in the parasitologist, reflecting the department's increasing focus on things microscopic, and chose him by a majority vote. But the chairman argued that Kroodsma was the better candidate. The argument lasted an entire year, and in the end, the chairman appointed Kroodsma against the wishes of much of the department. "That was the beginning of the end of my career at UMass," said Kroodsma.

During this same stretch of years, Kroodsma stirred up a controversy far beyond the university. In 1986, he organized a workshop on "experimental design" at an American Ornithologists' Union meeting in Arizona. Several people at the workshop spoke about flaws in the design of experiments created to test hypotheses related to avian bioacoustics. The workshop was sparsely attended, and each presentation dealt with only part of the problem. Sitting at the airport on his way home, Kroodsma began to write a commentary. A year later he published his thoughts in *The Auk*. It was a simple, straightforward discussion of the methodology used in much of the current fieldwork, including some of Kroodsma's, and an analysis of various flaws in that methodology. Kroodsma's tone was neutral, and he used a hypothetical experiment involving a study of blue-winged warblers to illustrate the flawed methods. Although the experiment he criticized was hypothetical, the methods were real and were used by many of Kroodsma's colleagues. In effect it called into question the validity of many years of work and some of the conventional wisdom on birdsong.

Surprisingly, the reaction to this commentary, Kroodsma felt, was an indifference that suggested it hadn't been taken seriously. His response was to write a second commentary, but this time he would name names and cite specific studies that he felt were based on these flawed methods. Marler, with whom Kroodsma discussed the proposed paper, advised him against this approach, saying people would fight back because their backs would be against the wall. Some colleagues pleaded with Kroodsma not to include their names. Kroodsma wrote the paper. "Suggested Experimental Designs for Song Playbacks" devoted much of its attention to an experiment design problem known as pseudoreplication, a flaw that Kroodsma found all too common in avian bioacoustics research.

Once again, Kroodsma described a hypothetical experiment involving playback: "Suppose one wanted to test the following relatively simple null hypothesis. Male rufous-sided towhees . . . in Amherst, Massachusetts, respond no differently to songs of the local (red-eyed) population than to the songs of a specified white-eyed population from southern Florida." Kroodsma imagined a field experiment in which the researcher would prepare one tape recording of a "typical" song from a male towhee from Amherst and a second tape of a "typical" song from a male towhee from Florida. He would then play each of these two tapes to twenty different towhees in Amherst to see how they responded. If all or nearly all of the twenty birds responded the same way to each tape, it would seem to support the conclusion that the Amherst towhees responded the same to the two different songs. The researcher might assume that this is a statistically significant result because he tested twenty birds in his experiment. But wait, Kroodsma said, this isn't right. The conclusion is based on flimsy evidence. This is pseudoreplication. Testing twenty birds doesn't provide twenty examples at all. There remained only one example because only one song from each population was played.

When Kroodsma first explained this to me, I was confused by the logic. "Well, think of it this way," he said. "Say you want to find out if, as the old hair-coloring ad says, blondes have more fun. You follow one blonde around for a week and one brunette, and each has several experiences that indicate that blondes have more fun, so you conclude that, yes, blondes really do have more fun. But anyone would recognize the fallacy here—that you've only established this for one blonde." It was no different for the hypothetical experiment with the towhees. The hypothetical researcher "followed" only one song from Amherst around as it was introduced to twenty different birds, then followed only one song from Florida around the same way. One song may have gotten the same response from twenty different birds, but that would be no more statistically significant than the fact that one blonde got the same response from twenty men. And yet researchers frequently used this method, and then when they put together their chart of supporting statistics, they noted they had twenty examples rather than one. Thus, one example became twenty: it was falsely replicated—pseudoreplication. The original hypothesis, Kroodsma noted in his paper, referred to male towhees responding no differently to "songs" (plural)—not "a song."

The temptation the researcher gave in to was to say that the one song he selected for each of the two populations was typical, or representative, of the population because it sounded like other songs from that same population. Furthermore, the two songs from the two different populations clearly sounded different. On the surface this seems reasonable. It's easy for us to recognize that not all blondes are alike, and that any one blonde would not be representative of all blondes. We readily recognize these differences in other members of our own species. Might not the birds also readily recognize differences in individual songs of other members of their own species? One particular song may be sung slightly more forcefully, or subtle differences in tone may exist. Background noise on a tape may have an effect as well. There were, in fact, published reports that had noted birds responding to just such subtle variations.

This time, researchers fired off replies to Kroodsma's paper, defending their work and questioning his logic. The tone of some of the replies was less than collegial. William Searcy, whom Kroodsma had known for years, wrote a commentary in the following issue of *Animal Behavior* in which he defended his research. Kroodsma didn't give an inch. His reply to Searcy appeared in the same issue: "I wish I could agree with Searcy. . . . Knowledge would be gained more quickly, more easily, and more cheaply. . . . I do not concede, however, because Searcy's arguments are unconvincing and simply wrong." Kroodsma then summarized the danger of reaching conclusions too easily: "We 'know' that large song repertoires are more stimulating than small repertoires. We 'know' that birds of a given dialect will respond differently (probably more strongly) to songs of their own dialect than to songs of other dialects. We 'know' too much. Too often we therefore do experiments and are satisfied with finding results that are merely consistent with (but do not actually test) our preconceived knowledge and intuition."

Kroodsma was still immersed in these troublesome years when I first met him in 1995 on Martha's Vineyard, but he didn't mention any of this until much later. "That was a painful period for me," he told me. "I knew what I was getting into when I wrote those papers. Marler advised me not to do it. 'Lead by example,' he said. 'Do the right thing and others will too.' But I didn't think it worked that way. I guess I went for the jugular. The reason this bothers me so much is that I think the work is important, and it's important to do it right. And it's not about the people doing it; it's about the animals. Too many people are churning out publications to make themselves look good and to get grants. Some of the work that's done these days is more self-promotion than science."

What, after fifty years of research, do we really know? Our understanding of songbirds begins with anatomy, something that came to mind one afternoon as I talked to Kroodsma about his study of the Bewick's wren. In the middle of discussing his research, Kroodsma stopped momentarily to recall one particular morning when he'd stood and watched a wren perched on the tip of a branch at the top of an oak tree. The sun was just rising over the hills beyond the tree, silhouetting the wren against a pale sky. In the cold dawn air, the wren poured out song after song, each accompanied by a little puff of exhaled breath. Kroodsma stood and admired the scene: the wren, tail cocked, head thrown back with each song, his tiny body quivering—a beautifully etched cameo in the morning sky. How had evolution led to this moment? The wren was small enough that he could easily fit in one's shirt pocket. He weighed no more than the pen Kroodsma used to write his notes. His song, which carried upward of a quarter mile, was produced by vocal cords that would fit in a raindrop and were controlled by a brain that weighed one twenty-eighth of an ounce. Yet the wren repeated a complex series of musical notes with precision and force, warning any potential interloper that these trees and bushes were his and his alone.

Each time he sang, the wren expelled air from his respiratory system with extraordinary efficiency. Nearly 100 percent of the air passing through a bird's vocal cords is used to make sound. Humans use only about 2 percent. Exactly how a bird produces its song, however, is still not entirely understood despite decades of research. Anatomy was one of the first aspects of birds to be studied, and the knowledge that birds produced sound differently from humans appears, as one writer put it, "to be lodged in antiquity for it depends on the rather gruesome observation that ducks, geese, and chickens will continue their cries for some time after their heads have been cut off." This is to say that the bird's vocal organ is not at the top of its windpipe, the trachea, as is the case with the human larynx. Birds do have a larynx, but it serves only to close off the respiratory system when they eat. Another organ, located deeper in the body at the junction of the trachea and the bronchial tubes, produces sound. To eliminate the confusion from referring to an upper and lower larynx, a nineteenth-century scientist proposed that this vocal organ be referred to as the syrinx, from the Greek for "pipe," as in panpipe. (Syrinx was the mountain nymph whom the gods protected from Pan's lust by transforming her into a reed, from which Pan, ever ingenious, made a panpipe that he could put to his lips and play.) Early naturalists were reasonably certain that the syrinx produced birdsong, but no one knew how. In their speculation, they regularly compared it to a musical instrument. Its membranes were "shaped and arranged much like the double reed of the oboe," said one. Others described it as "a reed pipe," or as producing sound "in the same manner as in wind instruments, such as horns and trumpets."

It was easier to describe the parts of the syrinx than to explain how they operated. At the point that a bird's two bronchial tubes converge with the trachea lies a small air sac. This air sac, the membranes that form its walls, and the membranes, cartilage, and muscles attached to it are all parts of the syrinx. The syringeal muscles, which, in pairs, control movement, vary in structure and arrangement among the families of birds. Ostriches, vultures, and cormorants, surviving members of primitive groups of birds, have the simplest structures. The turkey vulture has no syrinx at all. Geese have one pair of syringeal muscles. Most nonpasserines have two pairs. Parrots have three. Songbirds generally have five to seven pairs, one of the anatomical traits that distinguishes the oscines from other birds. On the medial wall of each bronchus is a thin membrane. This tympaniform membrane, as it's known, vibrates like the skin of a drum as air forced from the bird's respiratory system passes it. Or so went one theory. Another theory asserted that these two membranes expanded to nearly close off the bronchial tubes so that air is forced through a small opening as in a whistle. How the sound is affected as it rises through the trachea and issues from the bird's beak is another matter. For a century biologists have tried everything they can think of to determine how the syrinx works. They've dissected it. They've severed the nerves that were connected to it. They've placed singing birds in helium-enriched chambers to understand how the trachea alters sounds produced in the syrinx. Breakthroughs came and went, replaced by new breakthroughs.

In 1933, Werner Ruppel, a German biologist, removed the syrinx from a herring gull and suspended it in an airstream, observing that the tympaniform membranes did indeed vibrate and produce sound, giving credence to the syrinx-as-a-drum theory. The next breakthroughs were derived from the physics of sound waves rather than the anatomy of the syrinx. In 1947, R. K. Potter analyzed a sonogram and noted that two independent sounds were occurring simultaneously, a finding supported by Donald Borror in 1956 with a sonogram of a wood thrush. The thrush's song contained harmonically unrelated notes that overlapped in time. This could only be explained if the notes arose from two separate sources at the same time. This suggested the thrush was, in effect, singing a highly synchronized duet with itself by producing sound in each of its bronchial tubes separately. The "two-voice theory," as this came to be known, was taken up in the 1960s by Crawford Greenewalt.

Greenewalt, a chemical engineer by training and president of the DuPont chemical company for a time, happened upon birdsong by way of his interest in photography, which itself was a by-product of his interest in orchids. Using photography to document the growth of his orchids led him eventually to the orchids of the bird world—hummingbirds. After designing a system to photograph hummingbirds that would freeze their wing action, he chanced upon the issue of bird anatomy and sound production in his casual reading on birds. When Greenewalt set out to investigate the problem of how the syrinx produced sound, and in particular whether a bird produced sounds independent of each other from the two halves of the syrinx, he took an engineer's approach. He reasoned that if he could analyze a bird's song in more detail than was currently possible with the sonograph, he should be able to determine if the sound waves were coming from one source or two. Greenewalt modified a sonograph and joined it to an oscilloscope, a wave analyzer, a timer, and a system of filters. He called this contraption, a box the size of a chest of drawers, a "signal analyzer console." When he fed recorded birdsong into it, the analyzer produced a detailed image of the sound waves.

Greenewalt was methodical. He produced sonograms for dozens of species, not limiting himself to songbirds. He began with some of the most primitive of birds, the common loon and western grebe. Then he went on to the vocalizations of ducks, hawks, owls, grouse, curlews, and dowitchers, working his way toward the most advanced of birds, the passerines. Here, he used his signal analyzer on more than forty species, including the eastern kingbird, tree swallow, tufted titmouse, pygmy nuthatch, rock wren, brown thrasher, robin, wood thrush, loggerhead shrike, white-eyed vireo, parula warbler, western meadowlark, red-winged blackbird, brown-headed cowbird, cardinal, American goldfinch, and white-crowned sparrow. This revealed that overlapping nonharmonic notes existed in nearly every family of birds he analyzed. Even the eared grebe produced such notes, as did the bittern and greater yellowlegs. Among passerines he found two voices in the gray-cheeked thrush, American goldfinch, green jay, catbird, Leconte's sparrow, song sparrow, Lapland longspur, and the wood thrush, the "most versatile and accomplished 'internal duettist,'" he said. The images he produced showed conclusively that some of the sounds were not related harmonically. In other words, they included frequencies that were not multiples of each other as they would be if they came from the same source. The conclusion was inescapable: they were produced by separate sources. It was astonishing—a bird singing a duet with itself. It seemed like something from a fable, no less fantastic than a bird rising from its own ashes.

Greenewalt knew his work was a significant contribution to avian bioacoustics, but he acknowledged its limits. To be honest, he said, this was nothing more than circumstantial evidence. To know for certain how the syrinx worked, one would have to watch it in action. And that seemed unlikely, he noted, given the placement of the syrinx deep in the body, its small size in songbirds, and, allowing himself some humor, "the extreme unlikelihood of producing a cooperative attitude in the subject."

Cooperative or not, birds were subjected to more anatomical experiments. In 1971 Fernando Nottebohm published the results of an experiment in which he cut the nerves that affected the right and left halves of the syrinx in canaries and chaffinches. Cutting the right nerve had little effect on the birds' songs, but when he cut the left, the birds were unable to sing properly. The most sophisticated and convincing experiments were performed by Roderick Suthers at the Indiana School of Medicine in 1990. Suthers was able to do what Greenewalt had imagined impossible—"watch" the syrinx in action. Suthers implanted miniature pressure sensors in the syrinxes of canaries, catbirds, and thrashers to measure the airflow in the left and right bronchial tubes as it passed by the tympaniform membranes. Both the catbird and thrasher produced independent sounds from the two sources. Some units of sound came only from the left bronchus, others only the right, and still others both simultaneously. Later studies with cardinals revealed they use the left and right branches sequentially to produce the pure whistled tones that range from 1 to 7 kilohertz. The left bronchus produces sounds below 3.5 kilohertz, and the right above that range. The result is a seamless whistle. Other studies showed that the cowbird alternates from one side to the other for its abrupt shifts in frequency. Ongoing studies, however, continue to produce results that indicate there's more to be learned. One recent experiment undermined the prevailing belief that sound was produced when the tympaniform membranes, extended into the airflow, vibrated. A bird whose membranes were rendered inoperable continued to sing normally. The latest theory is that different membranes are at work, the medial and lateral labia, which, when extended, produce a slit that air is forced through.

The study of song-learning in birds has begun to alter the long-held image of birds as unintelligent creatures of instinct (though *birdbrain* is still synonymous with *bimbo*). If a bird can learn an intricate song and reproduce it, to say nothing of controlling the two halves of the syrinx independently, it must have substantial brainpower. How the brain controls song has received as much attention as how the syrinx operates, and neurobiologists have made a number of discoveries in the last few decades. They have begun to map the song-control centers of the brain and the neural pathways that connect the brain to the nerves controlling the syrinx. The pathways are complex, and no one fully understands the neurological processes involved as birds sing, but locating the song-control centers allows biologists to conduct experiments that illustrate the brain's relationship to singing behavior. Fernando Nottebohm, another of Peter Marler's former students and one of the leaders in the field, discovered that two of the song-control areas in male canaries and zebra finches were three times larger than those in females. Since males sing and females don't, this might seem unsurprising, but in fact the prevailing wisdom at the time was that neurological differences between the sexes do not exist in vertebrate animals. Nottebohm also demonstrated that a canary's song repertoire had a positive correlation with the size of these song-control areas in the forebrain. Other studies revealed that the song nuclei in birds in breeding condition are 70 percent larger than in nonbreeding birds. Thus, changes occur in the brain from season to season.

Most studies of this sort have involved the canary and zebra finches. Nottebohm, who still works at Rockefeller University, made arguably his most important discovery in the early 1980s. A study on chickadees indicated that they produced new neurons in the area of the brain involved with memory (Nottebohm was wondering how chickadees remembered during the winter where they had stored seeds). But Nottebohm knew adult animals do not produce new brain cells. Brain cells, everyone agreed, were produced only in embryo. Once lost, they could not be replaced. That was basic neurobiology. Nottebohm continued his experiment anyway. He injected a radioactive marker into the brains of canaries every day for a week. He waited a month, killed the birds, then looked at the neurons from different areas of the brain. The marker he injected was a hydrogen molecule attached to thymidine, a chemical needed for cell division. If new cells were being created, they would display the hydrogen marker. To Nottebohm's amazement, he found abundant marked cells in the brains he inspected. The birds appeared to be producing new brain cells. When he presented his findings at a conference in 1984, the reactions ranged from skepticism to disbelief. Then the world's leading authority on animal brains refuted his findings. Nottebohm's work was virtually forgotten until several years later when another researcher found the same production of new brain cells in rats, then in tree shrews, and finally in marmosets. Her work too was met with disbelief. Eventually, though, the evidence piled up, and others conducted experiments with similar results.

Neurogenesis, the production of new brain cells, is now one of the most closely watched fields of neurobiology. It has great potential benefit to those suffering degenerative conditions such as Parkinson's disease, multiple sclerosis, and Alzheimer's. This is the kind of unexpected discovery that the National Institutes of Health and the National Science Foundation pin their hopes on when they provide millions of dollars each year for studies in neurobiology, biochemistry, and molecular biology—and little to the study of ecology and animal behavior.

Given the complexity of bird songs, it seems to follow that avian hearing must be exceptional. Why would birds produce intricately structured sounds if they couldn't hear the details? Historically, understanding auditory perception in animals has been the province of psychologists in the field of animal psychophysics. Inquiry has involved training birds to respond to stimuli in highly controlled laboratory experiments. The research has taken all kinds of approaches to the question of what birds hear and how the avian brain processes information, including experiments that seem both inspired and whimsical. Pigeons, for instance, have been invited to listen to excerpts from both Bach's Toccata and Fugue in D Minor and Toccata and Fugue in F for organ and Stravinsky's *Rite of Spring* for orchestra. And it turns out that some pigeons can distinguish between the two composers 90 percent of the time. They also "classified" Bach, Stravinsky, and several other composers in much the same way as human subjects did in the same test. Most experiments, however, have focused on the frequency range in which birds perceive sound and the degree to which they separate out discrete units of sound of short duration.

In *Bird Sounds and Their Meaning,* published in 1977, Rosemary Jellis summarized the conclusions of early studies: "[Birds] are capable of a far more accurate separation of sounds arriving in rapid succession, or, to put it another way, they have a better time resolution—probably as much as ten times better than ours. Many sounds which we hear as single notes, or perhaps as a vibrant noise, are now known to consist of a sequence of separate sounds and can be perceived by a bird in this way. . . . The visual equivalent of this ability would let us see a moving film as the series of still pictures from which it is composed. Aurally it means that more information can be conveyed in a short sound signal. This is probably why even the most extensive bird songs seem so brief to us. The bird with its speeded up time sense must feel as if it had sung its equivalent of an operatic aria." This appealing analogy satisfies the common perception that birds are able to hear the smallest details in their songs, something that even the sharpest and most trained human ear cannot pick up. How else could a young bird duplicate so precisely the songs it heard from an adult?

Laboratory experiments beginning in the 1980s, however, could not confirm this. Robert Dooling, a colleague of

Kroodsma's at Rockefeller University in the 1970s and presently a professor of psychology at the University of Maryland, is one of the leading researchers in the field. In 1982, he summarized the results of the most recent and precise tests, which indicated that birds and people have a similar hearing capacity. The tests showed people actually hear better across a broader range of frequencies than most birds. But from 1 to 5 kilohertz, where birds are most sensitive, they can detect changes in frequency as little as 1 percent. In other words, birds can discern a change in sound from 1,000 hertz to 1,010 hertz, a minute change. Still, Dooling discovered, humans were able to detect such changes too. Tests also determined that birds could not detect changes in a sound's intensity any better than humans could. Possibly the most critical aspect of hearing involves temporal resolution—being able to distinguish discrete units of sound that last only milliseconds (the still frames of the film in Jellis's analogy). These are the small elements of song that one can see on a sonogram. Dooling's tests demonstrated that here too birds did no better than people, though the results were impressive for both. Birds and humans can distinguish sounds as brief as two hundred to three hundred milliseconds. Though he stuck by his results, Dooling wasn't satisfied. In his summary, Dooling noted, "For most students of vocal communication in birds, a nagging question remains. How is it that we are unable to 'hear out' all of the subtle details seen in the sonogram of a complex vocalization when there is clear evidence from song-learning experiments that birds can learn to imitate these differences?"

I called Dooling one morning and asked about this "nagging question." First, he made a point about our tendency to too easily attribute unique powers to animals. "It's nice to be mystified that we're not hearing the fine detail in birdsong and the birds are, but I think in a way it's not too surprising," he said. "If you look at the fine details of human speech, it's amazing that we can learn and duplicate it. When we learn our mother tongue, we can perceive it efficiently, but when I'm listening to French, for instance, it's a whole different ball game. I perceive it as speech, but I don't understand any of what's going on. I don't have any sense of the nuances of it. My production system doesn't produce it, and my auditory system isn't tuned to it. Birds are doing something special with birdsong, but humans are also doing something special with human speech."

Nevertheless, Dooling has continued to test bird hearing, improving the design of his experiments year by year. Like those in avian neurology, he works primarily with budgerigars, the tiny Australian parrot we know as the parakeet, and with zebra finches. Birds are tested in a small wire cage that sits inside a soundproof chamber. The cage sits on the floor of the chamber, a small video camera suspended above it in one corner and a speaker connected to a computer directly overhead. On one side of the cage is a perch and a food tray. Food is dispensed when the bird pecks one of two sensitive microswitches. The birds are trained to peck the correct switch when they hear a change in the sound from the speaker, and once a bird is trained, it can be used for years in a variety of audio perception studies. Over the years Dooling tested hundreds of birds in thousands of trials. He computed the results, always with built-in control tests to be certain the birds weren't simply guessing which switch to peck. He approached the problem from every angle he could think of, and over and over he came up with the same results—birds and people hear equally well.

"Don Kroodsma always says to me, 'How is it that I listen to birds in the woods, and I come back and slow down the tape recording and I can hear stuff that I can't hear at normal speeds? How come you can't find out what these birds are doing?' Kroodsma and I have had these debates for years."

Only a few weeks later, Dooling came up with evidence that birds do in fact hear better than people. One of the difficulties in testing a bird's hearing is that changing one element of sound usually affects other aspects of it. So one cannot be certain which element the bird is responding to. Dooling tried to solve this problem in various ways over the years. Recently he discovered a way to create two waveforms using harmonic complexes that changed only the temporal fine structure in the sound. On this test the birds were three to five times better than people at discerning the fine structure. "It's a quirky test," Dooling said, "but I'm now convinced that it is true that birds can hear stuff in their vocalizations that we don't hear, and we have this evidence for it. For years I didn't believe it, but now I do."

In the five decades since William Thorpe captured his first baby chaffinches and brought them into the soundproof chambers at the Madingley Field Station, the subject of how birds learn their songs has become one of the most studied phenomena in animal behavior. Avian bioacoustics has produced a literature so large and diverse, it is dizzying to contemplate. Yet what we know with some degree of certainty is fairly modest. To begin with we must admit that of the forty-five hundred species of songbirds on the planet, biologists have studied song in only about three hundred of them. Of the one thousand species of suboscines, significant research exists for fewer than a dozen. These figures are not increasing rapidly. There is an incentive to stick to the species others have worked on because it is easier to build on a foundation than to start from scratch.

Current research acknowledges the most fundamental distinction we can make: we know that oscines learn their vocalizations—though this learning occurs in various ways and to varying degrees in different species—and we know that suboscines and other birds do not learn to vocalize, except for two notable exceptions. Some parrots and their relatives (birds in the order Psittaciformes) learn vocalizations, as do some species of hummingbirds. These exceptions tell us that song-learning evolved more than once—since songbirds, parrots, and hummingbirds come from different evolutionary lineages—though only the oscines developed the kind of vocalization we call songs. We know also that songbirds learn their songs, but not their calls, which are innate. Eastern and western meadowlarks, for example, learn each other's songs where the two species meet and hybridize in the Great Plains. But their calls do not change, which is one way to identify the eastern from the western birds. Exceptions exist here as well: goldfinches apparently learn their calls, and interestingly, the calls of paired birds match precisely.

We know that song is related to the male's desire to defend a territory and attract a mate. The most basic observations suggest as much. In temperate zones male birds begin singing in the spring when they are establishing territories and mating, a correlation that is hard to ignore. In addition, we know that males of some species typically sing less often once they pair up with a female, while unpaired males sing all day. Often, a paired male that loses his mate resumes singing as fervently as before. This kind of circumstantial evidence isn't enough for science. In pursuit of hard evidence biologists have conducted a range of experiments. They have sneaked into a bird's territory and played taped renditions of his species song to see how he reacts to what he perceives to be another male (much "wing quivering" and "aggressive trilling" along with an aggressive approach of the tape recorder). Others have captured male red-winged blackbirds, rendered them voiceless, then placed them back on their territory to see how their next-door neighbors respond to the sudden silence (they quickly attempt to take over the muted male's territory despite its obvious physical presence). To show that sex hormones are involved in song production, researchers have castrated male birds, noted that they cease to sing, then given them "testosterone replacement therapy." The birds begin singing again. In fact, testosterone injected into females often induces them to sing like males.

Some females don't need any help. In North America, female bluebirds and red-winged blackbirds sing, as do female mockingbirds, northern orioles, cardinals, black-headed grosbeaks, and white-crowned sparrows among others. Female mockingbirds sing on nonbreeding territories during the winter. A female black-headed grosbeak sings an abbreviated song when she is on the move with her fledglings. Of more interest, a black-headed grosbeak has been observed singing a song indistinguishable from the male's song when the male was away from the nest for an unusually long time. This led the researcher to wonder if the female was singing to trick the male into returning to defend his territory from a trespassing male. Female red-winged blackbirds wouldn't have much luck with this strategy since the males are polygynous. Although they mate with several females, they pair up with only one, leaving the others on their own. Thus, many red-winged blackbird females defend their nesting territories by themselves, using one of their two songs exclusively to repel other females.

We know that our basic definitions of song and call work most, but not all, of the time. Cedar waxwings, for instance, make no sound that we would think to call a song, though they are songbirds. Some birds that are not songbirds deliver musical vocalizations we certainly find pleasing. Bobwhite quail and loons come to mind. We know that *song* and *call* are troublesome terms when it comes to the black-capped chickadee. The chickadee's "gargle" call is more complex than its song. To complicate matters further, dialects occur. The vocalizations of the crow don't fit the categories very well either. Their rarely heard songs—unmusical clicks, rattles, caws, and coos—are produced when they're in close contact with other crows, a trait usually associated with calls. But their calls—loud caws—are reserved for broadcasting territorial rights. We know these questions of function can become even messier. Some birds, it seems, have impure intentions when they vocalize. In the tropics, flocks of different species often forage together, and some flocks consist of those same species year-round. We know that in one of these "mixed species flocks" the white-winged shrike tanager is almost always the first to give an alarm call if a predator appears. Thus, the flock is accustomed to the tanager acting as a sentinel. The birds respond accordingly. But now and then a tanager gives a false alarm, distracting another bird from an insect the tanager has also spotted.

We know that songbirds develop their songs in stages. Young birds hear their species song (or songs) while still nestlings and begin memorizing it early in life, though they make no immediate attempts to vocalize. We know from experiments that they seem to understand instinctively which sounds to memorize based on an innate species "song template" in the brain, ignoring the songs of other species they hear around them. (The heartbeat of a young song sparrow increases when it hears its species song for the first time, but remains unchanged in the presence of other sparrow songs.) We know that a bird's first attempts to produce sound, which typically begin soon after it has fledged, amount to nothing more than incoherent babbling. In this subsong, as it's called, many of the proper sounds are produced, but they're jumbled and incomplete. Researchers have often seen fledglings in the laboratory practice subsong immediately after being fed. They sit still and appear to be in a trance, their eyes closed, head tilted to one side, as they whisper sounds so quietly they're barely audible. If they are disturbed, they open their eyes and abruptly fall silent. We know that subsong may continue through the summer of the bird's first year, but by fall a young bird typically enters a silent period that lasts until late winter. As the days grow longer, it resumes its subsong practice sessions and within a few weeks begins to produce rough versions of its species song, called plastic song. By the spring of its first year, the new songster has usually perfected his "full song." We know that some songbirds continue to learn variations on the species song for a few weeks longer, adopting elements from the birds they encounter, while other species stop learning after they are only a few weeks old. Mimics such as mockingbirds and starlings of course go on learning throughout their lives.

We know that birds sing most spiritedly at dawn, perhaps to signal they made it through the night and still own their territory, or to catch the ear of females that have arrived overnight in migration. We know that many species sing from perches, but others from the ground or in low shrubbery. North American wood warblers that sing on or near the ground—ovenbirds, waterthrushes, Kentucky warblers—have the lowest-frequency songs of any birds in the family. This is an advantage since low frequencies travel better than high frequencies around obstacles such as tree trunks. Warblers that sing from low trees or shrubs—common yellowthroats, Wilson's warblers, yellow warblers—have songs that are higher-pitched, but not as high-pitched as the blackpoll, bay-breasted, and blackburnian warblers, which sing from the tops of trees where their short-wavelength songs encounter the fewest obstacles.

Most of all, we know that singing behavior varies greatly from one songbird species to the next, and often from one individual to the next. This variation is surely a consequence of learning, though that is not the same thing as knowing why it occurs. Two types of variation have attracted the most attention: a bird's repertoire (the number of different songs it sings) and the geographic variation that occurs among individuals of the same species, often as dialects. With regard to repertoires, we know that chipping sparrows, white-crowned sparrows, white-throated sparrows, savannah sparrows, lazuli buntings, indigo buntings, black-capped chickadees, common yellowthroats, ovenbirds, and veerys all sing only one song—if you don't count the flight songs given by the yellowthroats and ovenbirds. We know that the American redstart sings anywhere from 1 to 8 songs, the blue-winged warbler has 2 songs, the swamp sparrow sings 3 to 4 songs, Swainson's thrush 3 to 7, the eastern towhee 3 to 8, red-winged blackbird 2 to 7, western meadowlark 5 to 12, cardinal 8 to 12, Bewick's wren 10 to 20, and the western meadowlark 5 to 12. These are modest repertoires. Then there are birds with increasingly prodigious singing powers: the wood thrush—20 songs; starling—21 to 67; robin—100 or more; eastern meadowlark—50 to 90; Carolina wren—40. And then the true virtuousos: the western marsh wren with 150 to 200 songs, sedge wrens with 300 to 400 songs, mockingbird with 250, and the incomparable brown thrasher with 2,000 or more.

We know that of those species with repertoires, one song may be sung most frequently, while others are sung with varying degrees of frequency. And we know the order in which a bird sings its songs may vary. During the day, eastern towhees typically sing one song repeatedly, then go on to another in the repertoire and repeat it too before advancing to the next song, continuing this pattern until they have sung all of the songs in their repertoire. At dawn, however, the towhee runs through each of its songs immediately, one after the other, in less than half a minute. The former is called singing with "eventual variety," the latter singing with "immediate variety." We know that although the chipping sparrow has only one song, roughly thirty versions of it occur rangewide, and neighboring males rarely share the same version. Furthermore, the sparrows sing their dry rattle, a song that lasts about two seconds, throughout the day from an exposed perch high in a tree, pausing for about ten seconds in between songs. At dawn, male chipping sparrows from adjacent neighborhoods sometimes meet in small groups on the ground and sing abbreviated versions of their song in rapid-fire bursts, as if trying to gun each other down. We know that American redstarts, which may have anywhere from one to eight songs, have different habits yet. Birds with three or more songs will repeat one of their songs in a long singing "bout," but then sing the other songs one after the other. This is true as well of the yellow warbler and Grace's warbler. Song sparrows in the West cannot seem to sing the same song twice. Regardless of which song they are singing, they make minor variations from one rendition to the next.

As for geographic variation and dialects, we know the phenomenon occurs in nearly all the oscine species that have been studied, a sharp contrast to the suboscines and other birds whose innate songs are the same from one area to the next. In North America, the alder flycatcher's *fee-bee-o* is the same from the Atlantic to the Pacific, while, as Marler discovered, white-crowned sparrows in California only a kilometer apart may sing different versions of their song. For white-crowned sparrows the boundary between dialects is sharp. One can walk a short distance from one dialect group into another and hear a clear, immediate change in the dialect. More commonly the change occurs gradually. Carolina wrens in Ohio sing their songs faster than Carolina wrens in Florida. Theoretically, if one were to walk from Ohio to Florida listening to Carolina wrens, one could hear the songs slowing down along the way. Dialects are a consequence of young birds learning elements of their songs from birds in the area where they themselves will establish their territory and breed, something that has been documented for numerous species now. Although a young bird may have learned the basics of its song from its father, it makes adjustments to it after listening to adults in the area it has chosen for itself. As a result, neighbors often have similar songs. If the species has only one song in its repertoire, as is the case with the white-crowned sparrow, sharp boundaries may be established. When a bird has a repertoire, as the Bewick's wren does, it's more likely that neighbors will share many of their songs but not all. The possible permutations are staggering.

This is a portrait of avian bioacoustics painted with broad strokes. Variation within these birdsong basics is so great that a detailed account leads down a road without end. Much of the literature on repertoires and geographic variation is the result of time-consuming but relatively straightforward work. Documenting the number of songs an individual sings, establishing the repertoire of a species, or documenting the shared song dialects of one population in relation to others is as clear-cut as avian bioacoustics gets. Such work provides the base from which one can ask the big question: What functions do repertoires and dialects serve?

Most of the analysis and discussion of repertoires has circled one question: Does size matter? We know that the brown thrasher with its two thousand or more songs is no more successful as a species (it occurs in no greater numbers nor over no greater range) than the chipping sparrow with its one song. Thus attention has focused on how repertoires serve individual birds rather than the relationship of one species to another. Does a red-winged blackbird with five songs have advantages over a red-wing with three? One line of thought, based on studies with song sparrows and other species, is that a male can indicate how motivated he is in defending his territory or attracting a mate by how often he switches from one song to another. The more songs he has, the more often he can switch. Birds with large repertoires may be able to convey subtleties of meaning based on which songs they choose to sing at a given moment. Among neighboring males that share the same songs and countersing, as do cardinals, western meadowlarks, tufted titmice, and western song sparrows for instance, each bird can choose either to match his rival's song or ignore it and sing a different song from his repertoire. Countersinging may convey information regarding hierarchies of dominance and age (for sedentary birds, age indicates the number of years an individual has been on the same territory). This possibility seems particularly evident when countersinging birds deliver their songs in predictable sequences. Such behavior allows a bird to match the song his neighbor just sang or skip ahead and sing the next song in the sequence—in effect becoming the leader rather than the follower. The size of a bird's repertoire might also indicate his health. Studies with sedge warblers in Europe have shown that birds with larger repertoires have fewer parasites. Kroodsma's early work with the Bewick's wren illustrated a correlation between repertoire size and hatching date. Birds that hatched earlier in the summer, thereby receiving the benefit of more ample food supplies (and more time to practice singing before winter), had larger repertoires.

Much of the recent discussion on repertoires has an anthropomorphic echo to it. One study after another has asked if size matters when a male is trying to impress a female. Much of the literature appears to produce a clear answer: yes, a bird's singing prowess impresses the ladies. Those working in this field remind us that it is the female who selects the male, which suggests that females influence how males sing. A 1980 study of the polygynous red-winged blackbird demonstrated that males with larger repertoires had larger harems of females.

In addition, numerous laboratory experiments seem to confirm that females respond more favorably to males with larger repertoires. And a more recent study with the great reed warbler in Europe found a correlation between the size of a male's repertoire and his success in mating with additional females, and, more strikingly, the survival of his offspring.

Kroodsma and others, however, have pointed out problems with the studies. In the case of the red-winged blackbird, birds with larger repertoires were also older and had better territories than birds with smaller repertoires. Clearly these other factors may have been involved in their mating success. The laboratory experiments, which use taped songs played to live females, are both artificial and, often, statistically flawed—examples of pseudoreplication. In one case, a researcher who found that female song sparrows respond more vigorously to larger song repertoires could not duplicate his findings in field experiments with live males doing the singing. In addition, if evolution has favored birds with larger song repertoires, why then do so many species sing only one song, particularly when experiments have shown many species to be capable of singing additional songs? Skeptics of the studies do not suggest there isn't a relationship between repertoire size and mating success, only that there is scant unequivocal evidence to support it.

Song dialects have received as much attention as repertoires. Dialects got Thorpe and Marler thinking about birdsong in the first place. Hundreds of papers focus on the function of dialects, beginning with Marler's work with the white-crowned sparrow and his hypothesis that learning the local dialect isolated the sparrows genetically, thus speeding up evolutionary divergence and speciation. This possible link between dialect and speciation is still being debated and remains unresolved. The link between evolution and song-learning seems strong on the surface. Songbirds are the largest and most diverse taxon of birds on the planet. They also cover the globe and succeed in all kinds of habitats. Is song-learning—the suborder's most unique trait—somehow connected to this evolutionary success? It may only be coincidence. And until someone is able to present empirical evidence that makes a strong case for the relationship between dialects and genetic isolation, it remains coincidence. Marler's white-crowned sparrows seem to make the case, and some still believe they do. But ongoing studies raise doubts that the sparrows learn from their fathers and remain near their natal area.

One of the most interesting studies of dialect linked it with habitat. In Argentina, the chingolo, or rufous-collared sparrow, has a single song, and groups of birds share the same dialect just as white-crowned sparrows do. One phrase in the chingolo's song, its final trill, remains relatively constant across wide ranges, but then changes abruptly, sung faster or slower. Those studying the chingolo began to notice a pattern. The trill rate could be correlated to habitat—woodlands, plains, foothill brushlands, and mountain semideserts. Further studies revealed that this held true over vast stretches of Argentina, and, most interesting perhaps, that the chingolos in cultivated land sang the proper trill for forest habitat, which, in fact, occupied the area before the land was cleared. In some cases, the change from forest to farmland occurred as much as a hundred years before.

But no one has yet found a similar situation with another species, which is what one would expect if habitat were a significant factor in song variation. A pattern involving several species would make a compelling connection between dialect and function. In addition to genetic isolation and habitat selection, social adaptation is the other most frequently investigated link with dialects, and this is where Kroodsma has done most of his work. Kroodsma believes that the key to understanding dialects in songbirds lies with the chestnut-sided warbler. In 1978, he read a paper published by a friend, Ross Lein, which discussed the two song types of chestnut-sided warblers, an observation that was first noted in the literature in 1962 (a perfect example of why ornithologists tend to work repeatedly on the same species). Birders know the warbler's song as a rapidly delivered series of whistles with an emphatic penultimate note. The common mnemonic description is *pleased pleased pleased to MEETcha*. The warbler has a second different song as well, though. Peterson's *A Field Guide to the Birds of Eastern and Central North America* says simply, "Also a more rambling song." Ross Lein's paper observed that male chestnut-sided warblers sang *pleased pleased pleased to MEETcha* when they were interacting with females and their rambling song when they were debating property rights with other males—a rare case of the use of different songs for different functions.

Kroodsma began recording chestnut-sided warblers in the spring of 1979, but found himself drawn to blue-winged warblers as well, which also sang two different song types. In the years that followed, he began experimenting with the birds, playing a variety of the recorded songs to them to see how they reacted to different songs. He also raised baby warblers to understand how they learned their songs. In 1986, he devoted the birdsong season to the chestnut-sided warbler, driving each morning from his home in Amherst to the Berkshires and walking along a power line listening to the warblers packed into territories in the dense brambles that grew on the edge of the open ground. The warblers began singing about forty-five minutes before dawn, singing their warble song. Between songs, they uttered a series of simple notes, something like *chip chip chip chip chip chug-chug-chug*, according to Kroodsma's description. Near sunrise, all the males switched to *pleased pleased pleased to MEETcha*.

From his own work and the work of others before him,

Kroodsma put together a picture of the singing behavior of the warbler that shed light on the origin and function of dialects in songbirds. Early in the spring when the chestnut-sided warbler returns to its breeding grounds, it sings *pleased pleased pleased to MEETcha* repeatedly, averaging six songs a minute. But each male is like a "MEETCHA robot with a simple on/off switch," Kroodsma has written. Once he has paired up with a female, he sings his MEETCHA song far less frequently. Kroodsma tested the function of the song by removing female warblers from pairs and replacing them a couple of hours later. The males, robbed of their mates, began singing *pleased pleased pleased to MEETcha* again at the rate of six or seven songs per minute, then stopped just as abruptly when Kroodsma returned their mates. Clearly *pleased pleased pleased to MEETcha* had a lot to do with attracting a mate.

When Kroodsma began analyzing *pleased pleased pleased to MEETcha* songs with the sonograph, he discovered there were four basic versions of the song in the Berkshires. He compared these four songs with songs from other parts of the country and was startled to discover the warblers sang the same four songs everywhere. There was only one exception, a fifth song in northern Minnesota and Wisconsin. The uniformity was amazing. From tapes made of chestnut-sided warblers in the 1950s, it was clear the songs had not changed over time. There were no dialects of the song, as he had expected (since dialects occur in nearly all songbirds that have been studied over such distances). How had the warblers managed this feat? Did warblers from across the continent mingle during migration and hear each other sing, thus duplicating the same songs? It was a difficult question to answer. More important perhaps, why did the warblers share these same songs across their range? Kroodsma has an idea: "These are the songs a male uses to attract a female, and when he courts a newly arrived female, these are the songs that he whispers in her ear. Because female songbirds tend to move farther from their birthplace than do males, perhaps males are making sure that they have a MEETCHA song that will be recognizable to any female, regardless of her origin." Another idea came to mind as well: "A friend in Israel once said to me, 'Well, if you are auditioning opera singers and you want to pick the best singer, you give them all the same piece to sing, so you can compare them more easily.' So maybe that is what the females are demanding of the males."

Although the warblers sang the same few *pleased pleased pleased to MEETcha* songs throughout their range, Kroodsma and his colleague Bruce Byers, who continues to work with warblers, found that the rambling songs used for interacting with males varied tremendously. Each male sang up to a dozen "warbled songs," and neighboring males usually shared the same repertoire. Just a few territories away the songs were completely different. An almost infinite variety of warbled songs existed, but shared songs existed in small, highly localized dialect areas. Kroodsma knew from banding the birds that they returned each year to the same territory, so it made sense the birds were learning the warbled songs from their close neighbors. In Kroodsma's words, "natural selection has refined this form of singing so that neighbors speak the same tongue." Is this the best evidence yet as to why songbirds have dialects? That the warbler's *pleased pleased pleased to MEETcha,* the song used for female interaction, does not vary throughout the range and the warbled song varies greatly from one group of males to the next makes a convincing case for geographic variation as an aid to social interaction of males with other males.

A single case, dramatic as it may be, is a solitary example, not a pattern–but a pattern has begun to emerge. The blue-winged warbler also has two song types. One, used with females, varies little, while the other, used with males, varies greatly. Add to this the case of the black-capped chickadee, whose song is uniform throughout nearly all of its range, while its gargle vocalization, used in aggressive male interaction, varies geographically. And then add the case of the grasshopper sparrow with a similar pattern for its two song types. If one includes both warblers, closely related species, as one example, this provides three examples overall from three different taxonomic groups of birds. Kroodsma talks excitedly of this. It is possibly the key piece of evidence that explains the function of dialects in songbirds. On the other hand, Kroodsma is as skeptical of his own work as of others'. What are the odds that this pattern is just coincidence? "So far we've flipped the coin three times," he says, "and it's come up heads each time. The probability of that happening is one in eight, so it's not that uncommon. If we had five species rather than three, I'd feel better about this. There's only a three percent chance that the coin will come up heads five times in a row. That would be more convincing, less likely a coincidence."

When and if someone will find more species with similar singing behavior is impossible to say. Kroodsma's speculation awaits confirmation or rejection. Either one would be valuable. Although science is a process—curiosity that flows toward reason, ideas shaped by observation and experiment—it is also the slow accretion of knowledge. One study builds on another like grains of sand collecting at a bend in a river. Each grain of sand is an act of seeing. And for more than three centuries, what we know of birds—from anatomy to behavior—has been based, literally, on what we've seen. Whether with binoculars or a microscope, we've relied on our eyes to examine every facet of the lives of birds, but one. What will we know after we've listened to birds for three hundred years?

On the last day of May one year, I took a long evening flight from Florida to Nevada, arriving in Reno at midnight. The next morning, heading northwest, then west into California, I drove into the foothills that form the northern rim of Sierra Valley, a western spur of the Great Basin that juts like a jigsaw puzzle piece into the Sierra Nevada. Driving with the windows down, glad to have left the humid air of Florida behind me, I caught a fragment of the liquid song of a western meadowlark coming from the sage. It was gone at almost the same instant I heard it, as if swept behind me to stay in the hills where it belonged. But that snippet of song reopened the West to me, reminding me instantly of the six years I was a graduate student in Utah in the 1970s. There, western meadowlarks sang in the dry foothills next to our house, and now all the long afternoon walks I took in those foothills came flooding back to me. I remembered the blond and amber grasses, the prickly foxtails that clung like fishhooks to my socks, and the crumbling, rocky soil. I remembered the unfathomable blue sky that seemed like an ocean I would rise into when I reached the top of the first foothill, where I sat down and drifted away from my life as a graduate student. For me, birdsong often arrives as the bearer of memories, or of a particular landscape.

I followed the highway south through Sierra Valley, then west as it climbed into the mountains and crossed Yuba Pass. A few miles south of the pass, in Tahoe National Forest, I pulled into San Francisco State University's Sierra Nevada Field Campus and stopped at the main building, a two-story structure. On the upper floor, where the station's dining hall doubles as a classroom, I found Greg Budney, curator of the Macaulay Library of Natural Sounds. Budney was unpacking recording equipment from two dozen boxes lined up along one wall. Microphones, tape recorders, cables, earphones, and other gear were gathered into piles. Each year, usually at this field station, Budney leads a weeklong natural-sound recording workshop. The workshop attracts participants from throughout North America and as far away as Japan and Australia. Professionals who want to hone their recording skills attend as well as beginners. Katherine Payne, who has done groundbreaking work on the African elephant's use of infrasonic signals to communicate across great distances, is a workshop alumna, as is Sandra Gaunt of the Borror Laboratory of Bioacoustics.

The workshop is a microcosm of the world of natural-sound recording, and the attendees are typical of both the growing number of young scientists interested in bioacoustics and, equally important, the many nonscientists who contribute recordings to sound archives, thus providing researchers with the "vocal specimens" their work depends on. It is also a window into the fundamentals of natural-sound recording, an enterprise demanding attention to both audio electronics and natural history. Sixteen people had signed up for the workshop and would begin arriving the next day. Three came from other countries, Panama, Argentina, and Israel. For seven days, they would practice listening to the natural world and recording what they heard. The workshop focused on birds not only because most participants had come to record birds, but also because birds are conspicuous and accessible—they would be singing in every valley and on every slope. Participants would be immersed in birdsong from well before first light until they turned in at the end of the day. "It's sort of like boot camp, only we don't shave your head," Budney told the group the first day. Budney would be happy if the participants left at the end of the week with improved recording skills and good memories of the week, but it was a poorly kept secret that he hoped some would eventually become contributors to the LNS collection.

Although LNS has the largest collection anywhere (worldwide, the only comparable collection is the British National Sound Archive), thousands of species of birds are not represented. Furthermore, its collection of North American bird vocalizations, not surprisingly the strongest area in the archives, is far from complete when one considers how many different songs and calls exist for each species and how much variation occurs. It is vital to the library and to avian bioacoustics that the collection of bird songs continues to grow. Without such a collection, cataloged and accessible to scientists, much of the current research in bioacoustics would be impossible or agonizingly slow. Before Kroodsma visited the Library of Natural Sounds in 1994, his interest in the mystery of the chickadee's song had not gone beyond the stage of serious musing, but when he stood in one of the library's recording studios and listened to chickadees singing the reversed *sweetie hey* song, everything changed. It is hard to say what shape Kroodsma's investigation of the chickadee would have taken—or if he would have done anything at all—if he had not visited the library. And of course he would not have come across the *sweetie hey* song in the first place had not Dolly Minis been contributing her recordings of Martha's Vineyard birds to LNS.

Whenever he can, Budney entices a well-known expert to

spend a day or two at the workshop. The guest may give a talk about his or her work, but Budney knows it is simply the presence of an accomplished professional that can pay the most lasting dividends. Someone who can act as model and source of inspiration is what Budney has in mind. This year, Don Kroodsma told Budney he would stop in at the workshop for a few days on his way back to Massachusetts from a trip to the West Coast.

There's a camaraderie among those who record birds, whether they are scientists or not. They recognize that they are an eccentric lot–part naturalist, part electronic engineer. One must know the lives of birds; be eager to rise in the predawn darkness and spend the early-morning hours lugging around as much as thirty to forty pounds of equipment, pockets stuffed with batteries, cables, and tape cassettes; be inclined to spend the evenings cleaning tiny wheels and belts with cotton swabs; and be able to speak the language of hertz, decibels, sound attenuation, and tape bias. Budney's knowledge of recording equipment extends far beyond these fundamentals. He can parse the logarithmic ratio of the decibel, discuss the properties of various brands of tape, and describe the difference in polar patterns of cardioid, hypercardioid, and supercardioid microphones.

The real trick is understanding the relationship between bird behavior and the physics of recording equipment. Budney knows, for instance, that a certain color, texture, and pattern of bird droppings on one side of a downed tree trunk indicates the direction a ruffed grouse faces as he sits on his favorite platform. Perched there each day during breeding season, he makes his basso profundo booming to announce his presence to other grouse. To Budney, this means he can place a microphone a short distance in front of the deadfall and run a cable from it to his tape recorder a hundred feet away. Out of sight of the grouse, he has a chance to get a recording. His choice of equipment will not include a parabolic microphone system because the grouse's low-frequency sound waves (among the lowest in the bird world at around forty cycles per second) are twenty-eight feet wide—far greater than the diameter of a parabolic reflector. Sound waves this wide would spill over the edges of the dish. Therefore, Budney would use a shotgun microphone. Like Kroodsma, Budney is nothing short of fanatical when it comes to recording birds. He once convinced fellow recordist Randy Little to hang out the open door of a moving van to record a ruddy duck. The duck, in a slough parallel to the road, dove frequently, then called when it surfaced. With the car moving at the speed of the duck, Budney held on to the steering wheel with one hand and Little's belt with the other as Little leaned out the door and aimed the microphone, capturing the duck's vocalizations each time he surfaced.

Budney keeps track of much of what is going on in bioacoustics, and his knowledge of recording equipment and how to put it to use in the field is second to none. Budney, in his early forties, with sandy-red hair and a beard that partially conceals a ruddy complexion, did not set out to become an expert on recording birds. Unlike Kroodsma, Budney holds no advanced degrees. He is self-taught. Growing up not far from Ithaca, he majored in biology at the State University of New York at Geneseo and graduated with, in his own words, "little sense of direction." Budney took a job as a technician at the Library of Natural Sounds shortly after graduation while he considered graduate school and a career in waterfowl management. He spent his hours splicing tape, winding reels, and cataloging recordings going into the collection. To his surprise, something about being around sound-recording studios and hearing bird songs all day appealed to him. His attention to detail eventually caught the eye of James Gulledge, then curator of the library. In 1981 Gulledge asked Budney to help a young ornithologist named Ted Parker log his recordings into the library's archives. Parker, who was recording birds throughout South America, was fast becoming the world's leading authority on neotropical birds. Each year Parker would spend two or three weeks at LNS adding hundreds of recordings to the collection, and his studio sessions were notoriously long. Gulledge thought Budney could help Parker speed up the process.

"Here I was, a young lab tech who knew nothing about birds, asked to help the guy who knew everything about birds," Budney says. "Ted didn't like it at first. He thought I was slowing him down. I'd learned a lot of neotropical birds by hearing them so much, but I probably couldn't have identified three birds by sight. It was a pretty rocky start." Budney stuck with it, though, and eventually Parker must have recognized something special in Budney because he began urging him to get out into the field and do some recording himself. Within a couple of years, Parker was insisting that Budney meet him in Peru to see the birds he had only heard on tape. Parker in fact made arrangements for the trip and helped finance it.

By 1985, Ted Parker's knowledge of birds of the New World tropics was unparalleled and his ear for bird vocalizations simply uncanny. Parker could identify more than four thousand species of birds by sound alone. In the neotropics, Parker was the expert the other experts deferred to. Many thought of him as the greatest field ornithologist of the century. When I spent a couple of weeks in 1985 with Parker in northern Peru, he told me I had just missed meeting a young lab technician from Cornell. This lab tech, Greg Budney of course, had gotten a rude introduction to recording birds in the jungle, Parker said, when, loaded down with equipment, he slipped and fell into a spiny palm tree. Dozens of needlelike thorns had to be cut out of his hand with a razor blade. Undaunted, his hand bandaged,

Budney went on recording. "That trip turned my life around," Budney says. "Ted told everyone who'd listen, 'You've got to get out there and record while the birds are still there, before the forests are cut down. You can't wait.'"

When Budney was appointed curator of LNS in 1989, nearly fifteen hundred of the five thousand species of birds represented in the library's collection had been recorded by Ted Parker. In one of the great tragedies in twentieth-century biology, Parker died in 1993 at the age of forty in a plane crash in Ecuador. It was at his memorial service, held at the United States Botanical Gardens in Washington, D.C., that I first met Budney.

Budney spends most of his days in the LNS offices overseeing the day-to-day operations, which involve everything from cajoling biologists to contribute their recordings to the library to prioritizing the myriad requests the library receives, some personal as well as professional. Some years ago a nursing home asked for recordings of a nightingale for one of its residents, a 105-year-old woman who hadn't heard the bird's song since she was a young woman honeymooning in England. In the past decade institutions have increasingly recognized how sound can bring educational exhibits to life. Requests arrive frequently from museums, national park headquarters, and nature centers. Zoos request tapes as well. When the Bronx Zoo hoped to inspire romance in its long-tailed broadbills, a tropical bird, by playing for them some mood music of other broadbills, it contacted LNS. Hollywood producers call LNS too. *Forrest Gump* and *A River Runs Through It* are among the films that have acquired sounds from the library, and it was Budney who recommended a soundscape of chickadees, blue jays, and Canada geese to evoke a New England autumn for *Dead Poets Society*.

Nothing is more important to Budney, though, than the role LNS plays in conservation. LNS-produced audio guides, including those that accompany the Peterson field guide series, have helped countless birders learn to identify species by ear. If birders didn't have access to such recordings, we would know much less than we do about the population trends of North American birds. Every newspaper article that mentions a species in decline or the improved outlook for an endangered bird is getting information that relies largely on censuses like the annual North American Breeding Bird Survey. Administered since 1966 by the U.S. Geological Survey, this census employs volunteers throughout the continent to count birds they find along predetermined routes. Stopping for only three minutes at each point on their map, they often hear as many birds as they see. In recent years, LNS has created recordings specifically for such surveys. In the tropics, biologists who are racing to stay ahead of logging companies no longer have the luxury of taking months or years to survey the flora and fauna of potential biological reserves. Conservation International's Rapid Assessment Program, the brainchild of Ted Parker, has relied on LNS recordings in its fast-paced fieldwork to inventory a region's biodiversity. Birds are excellent indicators of a habitat's health and species-richness, and in lowland rain forests birds are much easier heard than seen. Taking this a step further, Conservation International and LNS recently collaborated to produce CDs that could be used to train local biologists in South America for census work. Each CD holds recordings of common birds of a particular habitat so, for instance, biologists can familiarize themselves with the songs of birds they are likely to encounter in a dry lowland forest before they survey such an area.

Other census work is focused on particular situations. Kathy Dunsmore, who works in the Bioacoustics Research Program next door to LNS, helped design a system of remote microphones to monitor the population of golden-cheeked warblers and black-capped vireos, both endangered species, on the firing and bombing range at Fort Hood in Texas, a site often closed to biologists for obvious reasons. Bill Evans, another associate of the Bioacoustics Research Program, discovered a way to use sound to census birds in migration. Evans positions a directional microphone along a migration flyway, points it at the night sky, and lets the tape roll throughout the night. Many migrating birds produce frequent call notes to keep track of others in a flock. Using software that the Bioacoustics Research Program developed to recognize the distinctive call notes of various species, Evans feeds his recordings into a computer that tabulates how many birds of each species passed over his site throughout the night. Evans imagines a time when he can set up an array of microphones at various sites and census bird populations this way from year to year. On the other end of the spectrum is the work of Stephen Kress, director of the Audubon Society's Seabird Restoration Program. Kress has been luring birds back to historical nesting grounds they abandoned due to human disturbance. Kress sets up speakers (along with decoys) and plays the sounds of large colonies of nesting birds to attract passing birds to the site. As a result, arctic, common, and roseate terns are once again nesting on Eastern Egg Rock off the coast of Maine, and dark-rumped petrels have returned to a nesting colony in the Galápagos Islands.

Now, as Budney stood in the field station's dining hall amidst piles of recording gear, his chief concern was organizing it. Budney and two of his co-leaders for the workshop, Randy Little and Dave Herr, both expert recordists, spent the afternoon unpacking boxes. Headphones went on one table, reels of cable on the floor, extension cords under another table. The room filled with recording equipment: several types of microphones, microphone windscreens, digital tape cassettes, thirty reels of BASF tape for reel-to-reel recorders, a half dozen state-of-the-art analog tape recorders, carrying cases to protect the recorders, and 150 D-cell batteries. The room looked like an espionage convention. The conversation was filled with acronyms: "We'll use the three AKGs. You wouldn't happen to have brought along a wind coat for an MKH 70?"

Budney has an ideal temperament—calm and unhurried—for tinkering with electronic equipment and waiting for unpredictable birds to burst into song. He gives the same attention to recording equipment as a dedicated fly fisherman gives to the flies he ties. Or perhaps it is the hours of moving slowly and deliberately in the presence of the birds he's recording that give him the purposeful approach for everything he does. In the years I've known him, I've seen him flustered only once, when, an hour down the road from where he'd spent the morning recording, he realized his watch was missing and remembered he had taken it off momentarily when we'd sat down to rest at the base of a fir tree. It was too late to turn back, he reasoned. But for the remainder of the drive he continued talking about the watch, unable to let go of the image of it lying among the fir cones and needles. "Someone is going to have a new watch," he said. A year later when I called him to talk about that day of recording, he remembered it as the morning he left his watch in the forest.

Budney, Little, and Herr sorted equipment throughout the afternoon and into the evening. By 9 P.M. we were all thinking of retiring for the night. The days would begin early, and though I could sleep in the next day while Budney, Little, and Herr drove to Reno to pick up the workshop participants, it was not too soon to begin making the adjustment to the hours we would be keeping for the next seven days. I followed the path through the trees to my tent, which I had set up next to the Yuba River. Earlier when I had talked with Budney by phone, he wasn't certain if there would be room for me in the field station's large tents, so I had brought along the old backpacking tent I've camped in for thirty years. Chronic back problems had dissuaded me from doing much camping in recent years, but now I was looking forward to going to sleep to the sound of the river and breathing the fragrance of firs and pines. With only the tent's thin membrane between me and the forest, I felt closer to the world than I had in some time.

When I rose the next morning the mountain air was crisp, the temperature in the upper thirties. We were at roughly six thousand feet, and at this time of year mornings were generally chilly, but the sun would eventually warm the mountainsides and temperatures would rise into the seventies by afternoon. Shortly before lunchtime, Budney and crew returned from the Reno airport with three rented minivans. Kroodsma would be arriving two days later. Of the sixteen people signed up for the workshop, four were young biology students with research projects that would rely in part on recording animal vocalizations. Susannah Buhrman, a new Ph.D. student at Cornell, would be working with parrots in Bonaire. Christin Khan, working on her master's degree at San Francisco State University, was interested in how harbor seals were able to locate their pups in a large group by their voices. Ashley Hayes, a young man working on a graduate degree at Idaho State University, was conducting research on the vocalizations of the American pika, that small relative of the rabbit found in the mountains of the West. Eduardo Bejerano, a student at Mount Hood Community College, was interested in using recordings for conservation projects in his native Panama.

The twelve other participants did not fit into any neat categories. An electrical engineer from New York hoped to use recordings of birds to document the biodiversity in a tract of forest he was trying to save from development. A woman from Minnesota designed natural history exhibits that used recorded sounds. A musician from California was creating computer programs that play music based on natural sounds. One participant, who was nearing retirement, wanted to record birds so he could add sound to the videos he made of his birding travels. A few had considerable experience with recording equipment and had come to hone their skills under the guidance of the best in the field. Others had little or no experience with tape recorders. Several people knew birds quite well, a few moderately well, but a number had virtually no experience. Budney wanted all of them to feel welcome. He had a sheet of paper in his pocket with their names and interests on it and had already begun to connect names and faces. To add to the challenge of keeping everything running smoothly, four people from National Public Radio would be arriving later in the day: *Morning Edition* reporter Alex Chadwick, producer Carolyn Jensen, and two sound engineers, Bill McQuay and Sean Fox. They would spend most of the week shadowing Budney and others in the field each day for a program on the natural-sound recording workshop.

After lunch, Budney stood at the end of the dining hall. He set out five new Marantz tape recorders that had been loaned to the workshop. "Whatever you do, don't use mosquito repellent when you're handling the equipment." Budney cast a mock-stern look at the group. "Deet takes the plastic right off the earphones, and if you touch the recorder with deet on your hands, your fingerprint will be on it and we'll track you down." Several people gathered around the table. "I'm going to go over the basics of using the recorders. It's probably too basic, but all the little things are important. One of the switches on these recorders makes it possible to record directly from a telephone line rather than from the microphone. It's easy to bump the switch. I won't even tell you about the Cornell grad student who went to Venezuela and didn't get any recordings because a switch was in the wrong position. People send recorders to LNS and say they don't work, and we flip a switch and send them back to them."

Budney went over each part of the Marantz recorders, pausing to emphasize the VU meter. "You have to know where the VU meter is and carry the recorder so you can see it easily. It tells you how much sound you're picking up. One thing to be aware of—this equipment, and all the equipment on the market, is not designed for use with birds. The needle of a VU meter takes three hundred milliseconds to move from an at-rest position to the high-amplitude position. Although that's a small fraction of a second, some birds produce calls of only five to ten milliseconds duration, so their peaks of sound won't register on a VU meter at all. You can check to make sure the meter is working by just snapping your fingers." Budney snapped his fingers and the VU meter needle jumped. Moments later, a dozen people were snapping their fingers next to their recorders.

An hour later, the group filed outside for a demonstration. On the forested slope behind the dining hall, Kathy Dunsmore, the fourth workshop leader, placed a tape recorder in a brush pile and turned it on. It played the song of a canyon wren. Dave Herr stood a hundred feet downslope with his recorder. "The first thing you want to do is make certain your headphones are *not* on your ears. It's easiest to locate a singing bird if you can hear with both ears. Then you want to decide the best way to approach the bird, which depends on the environment and the bird. If it's a bird I've never recorded, I'll start rolling tape right away so I can be sure to get something on tape, even if it isn't very good."

Herr was using a parabolic microphone system, which he

began sweeping back and forth, then up and down, to locate the "sweet spot," as he called it, the point at which the sound was loudest. "Now I'll record for one or two minutes, then halve the distance between me and the bird," Herr said. "Halve the distance, double the gain."

Herr continued the lecture by explaining how to record an announcement on the tape that would provide basic data about the bird recorded, the habitat, weather conditions, and so forth—all vital information to a scientist who might want to use the recording later in his research. "What happens if you don't know what bird you're recording," someone asked, followed by a second question before Herr could answer the first: "What if you don't even see the bird?"

"Well, that's a problem. But don't worry about that for now. Just do the best you can. Ask one of us if we're nearby," Herr said.

Budney spoke up. "You are all going to come away from the workshop with some great recordings. Maybe even something special."

"Hasn't it all been done already in North America?" someone asked.

Budney had been waiting for this question. "I can guarantee you that before the workshop is over someone here will record something no one has ever recorded before at this workshop. And that's just from recording in this one area. People send us stuff all the time at LNS that we don't have in the collection. There's still a lot to be done right here. You don't have to go to exotic places to get important recordings. You can get something in your own backyard. That sparrow that you hear singing every day near your house might just be singing a song no one has ever recorded before."

Budney's face was flushed with emotion. A short time later, after everyone had returned to the dining hall and, at Budney's request, each participant had formally introduced him- or herself to the group, Budney spoke again. "Working with people like you is what keeps me going. What you are doing is important." It's the kind of thing said at all kinds of workshops, and though Budney has no doubt been saying it year after year to each group, it seemed sincere.

Later, after dinner, Budney went over the daily routine. "Everyone has to be in the vans by five-ten A.M.," he said, eliciting several groans. "We'll drive to our recording site and begin recording by dawn each day. Tomorrow we're going to Dyson Lane in Sierra Valley. It's an open area, a marsh, so the birds are easy to find."

Knowing that getting out of a cold tent every morning and working with unfamiliar equipment could wear thin, Budney, Herr, and Little kept their talks light and provided some extra incentives. There was, for instance, the business of "milkshake birds." Herr had made several oblique references to this earlier, leaving people with quizzical looks. Now he wrote "milkshake birds" on a dry-erase board and listed several species: white-headed woodpecker, Lewis's woodpecker, black-throated gray warbler, band-tailed pigeon. "Get a recording of a white-headed woodpecker, and Greg will buy you a milkshake," Herr said. It turned out that a mile down the road was a general store with an old-fashioned ice cream counter. At the end of the week, all those who had recorded milkshake birds would get to line up at the counter and order what they pleased.

In what remained of the evening, Budney and the other leaders worked individually with those who needed help with their equipment. In one corner of the room, Budney huddled over a Nagra reel-to-reel recorder with Eduardo Bejerano, the young man from Panama. From the time the group arrived, Budney had shown a special interest in Eduardo, knowing that helping young Latin American biologists launch their careers would surely benefit the health of the New World tropics, where roughly one-third of the world's species of birds live. Eduardo had brought a tape recorder with him from Mount Hood Community College, but it was an old machine and not a very good recorder in the first place, so Budney suggested to Eduardo that he use the Nagra. Eduardo, a quiet, soft-spoken young man with a running back's build, was beaming with delight at the Nagra recorder.

"This is the kind of recorder Ted Parker used," Budney said.

In the age of small, lightweight digital tape recorders, the Nagra is like a big-finned car. It is legendary for its ruggedness and reliability in the field, which is why Parker would work with no other recorder on his long sojourns in lowland rain forests. Budney ran through the basics of the recorder with Eduardo, showing him how to load the reels of tape and attach one end of the tape to an open reel. He was still talking with Eduardo when I left the dining hall and walked back to my tent to retire for the day. As I turned downslope toward the river and walked through a group of fir trees, I heard the liquid notes of a hermit thrush from somewhere under the firs. In the dim light, I couldn't see the bird, but I didn't need to. The song was rich and musical, the flutelike notes shifting like the water flowing over rocks of the Yuba River.

The next morning, a little after 4 A.M., I crawled out of my tent to a starry sky and frigid air. At the dining hall, several people milled about with mugs of hot coffee cupped in their hands. Bundled up with wool hats, mittens, boots, and layers of shirts and sweaters, the group looked stunned by the cold, and at the moment it seemed hard to believe that it was June and birds would be singing exuberantly in less than an hour. By 5 A.M. people began loading their recording equipment into the vans. As first light seeped into the sky, we headed out, driving east up and over Yuba Pass, then descending into Sierra Valley and turning north. In thirty minutes, we turned east into the valley, passing several hot springs with vapors hanging above them. Mist was also rising from the waters of the marsh spreading out before us. The valley is agricultural land, and cows dotted the sage-covered plain. We stopped just past the springs and began unloading. The valley, a flat-bottomed bowl rimmed with low mountains, was a mix of two shades of green, the light green of sage, and the darker greens of sedges and marsh grasses. A few strung-out clouds hung in the east just above the horizon where the sun was rising. The early-morning light, a soft amber, spilled onto the mountains to the west, lighting up the dark green spires of pines.

Red-winged blackbirds, meadowlarks, and marsh wrens were singing nearby as people exited the vans, but the group hung together, waiting for instructions. Budney, dressed in blue jeans and a red Polarfleece jacket, stood before them and delivered the information they would need to record announcements on their tapes about the recording environment: "The elevation here is forty-eight hundred feet. We're in Plumas County. Don't forget to note that on your recordings. This is a good place to begin recording because we have essentially a two-dimensional environment—a flat plain. It's easy to see the birds, and easy to aim the mike at a bird here. The cows are the main undesirable noise. Be aware as you record where the cows are, and the other possible sources of noise. The highway is over there, and to the north is a railroad line." Before the group disassembled, Budney reminded them of something he had told them yesterday: "Remember, don't point a clear parabola into the sun. It will concentrate the light and cook your microphone. It'll happen quickly." He paused for effect. "If you happen to be looking at it, all you'll see is a little puff of smoke."

People slowly began to disperse, several stopping a few yards away where a marsh wren was singing boisterously. The wren was in cattails at the edge of the road, and unafraid, so he was an easy subject to record. I thought of Kroodsma's work on the western marsh wren and wondered if anyone here other than the LNS folks knew how many songs this wren had in his repertoire. There was no time to consider this though. People headed down the road, and a few slipped through a barbwire fence and walked out into the pasture where sparrows, blackbirds, and meadowlarks were singing in the sage. Budney turned his attention to Eduardo, who was fixing his microphone into its shock mount. Because people were beginning to record, Budney spoke in a whisper to Eduardo, suggesting they walk down the road. The NPR crew had decided to send one of the sound engineers, Bill McQuay, with Budney, so as Budney and Eduardo began down the road, McQuay followed closely in Budney's footsteps, holding a microphone on a short boom just over Budney's shoulder. Budney was too focused on helping Eduardo to consider the irony that someone was recording the recordist, and perhaps because he was so accustomed to being around recording equipment, he seemed hardly aware of McQuay's microphone dangling next to him.

Budney and Eduardo headed south, then turned west onto the main road leading into the area. A meadowlark singing in the distance caught Eduardo's attention. Budney reminded him how to sweep the microphone back and forth to locate the meadowlark and to keep the volume turned up to begin with so he would be able to pick up the meadowlark's song. Eduardo had all his attention focused on what he was doing as he pointed the mike at the distant bird and turned on the recorder. He recorded for a few minutes, then turned off the Nagra, aware the bird was too far away to get a clear recording. Budney offered encouragement: "You did a very good job setting your sound level." Eduardo smiled, then added an announcement to his tape, noting this was a recording of a western meadowlark in Sierra Valley, Plumas County, California, on June 2 at 6:14 A.M.

Moments later, Eduardo picked out a yellow-headed blackbird singing its hoarse, ratchety song from cattails near the edge of the road. This bird was much closer. As Eduardo prepared to record, Budney whispered more instructions: "Don't breathe too loudly. And don't move your feet to aim the microphone. Move your arm. We're on a gravel road and it will make noise if you're shifting your feet. Now watch for a slight movement in the tules. That's where he'll be. One thing we could do is kneel down so we won't be as threatening a figure to the bird." Eduardo was slow and purposeful in his movements, paying attention to each action. In between the songs of the blackbird, Budney asked, "What can we do to minimize the noise of those cows over there?" Eduardo moved a few feet and changed his angle on the birds. He continued recording, his face frozen in concentration. Budney, noticing that Eduardo's earphones were askew, reached over and gently repositioned them. After a few minutes of recording, Eduardo stopped, concerned that he had not gotten a good recording because the blackbird was hidden deep in the tules and cattails. "Recording with vegetation in your way is good practice for the forests in Panama," Budney said.

As we continued down the road, several ibis flew past us. "Those are white-faced ibis," Budney told Eduardo. "About the only time they make a sound is when they rise out of the marsh, and then they sound like a goose honking." Budney spotted another meadowlark, this one on a fence post along the road edge. He suggested that Eduardo try to record it, first from where we were standing, and then by moving closer. "Remember," Budney said, "halve the distance, double the gain." We should walk down the road, Budney explained, staying near the fence line so we were less conspicuous, then duck down when we got near the bird. He told Eduardo how to wear his headphones so he could put them on and off with one hand, a more efficient motion that wouldn't interfere with recording. Although it seemed that Budney was delivering a nearly constant series of instructions, he parceled out his advice, not saying too much at one time. And he kept what he said simple and direct, hoping not to overwhelm Eduardo.

After Eduardo recorded a few minutes of the meadowlark, we walked slowly toward the bird, drawing to within a hundred feet. Eduardo recorded again. When he finished, Budney offered more encouragement. "That was nicely done. I could hear the song coming out of your headphones. You did a good job." He suggested Eduardo review the meadowlark song, but play it back only through the earphones so the bird wouldn't hear it and be disturbed. Budney showed him step by step how to rewind the tape and replay the song. As he was doing this, a willet flew in and landed on a fence post across the road. The willet was close enough that Eduardo should have been able to get a high-quality recording, better than what he might have hoped for on this first morning out. There was a slight problem though. Before Eduardo could begin recording, he had to fast-forward the tape through the rest of the meadowlark recording. "Close the case," Budney told him. "It will make the machine quieter and won't disturb the willet." As soon as Eduardo had forwarded the tape, Budney spoke: "Don't wait for the willet to begin vocalizing before you turn the recorder on. You'll miss part of the call. Start recording right away." Eduardo aimed the microphone and turned the recorder on. The willet called several times over the next few minutes, once as another willet flew by. Eduardo kept the recorder running, watching his sound-level meter. When the willet flew off, Budney was pleased. "Now that was a great recording. A long sample. And no cows in the background. Most people don't do so well their first time out."

Budney decided it was time to work with someone else. He pointed out another bird to Eduardo, then wished him luck. Leaving Eduardo behind, he walked back toward the vans. Christin Khan was walking through the sage, apparently looking for something to record. "She has her microphone pointed at the ground," Budney said. "We'll have to fix that. She's accustomed to recording harbor seals, but she won't find any here." Budney stepped over the barbwire fence and headed toward Christin. We had been in the valley nearly two hours already. It was seven-forty-five, and the sun had begun to warm the air. As we approached Christin, Budney spotted a savannah sparrow landing on a low perch a hundred feet away. He pointed to the bird, then suggested Christin record him right away from this distance. We knelt down in the sage as she recorded, but Christin quickly realized that she was too far away. "Let's halve the distance, and try again," Budney said. "And watch the bird's behavior. Does he flip his tail when he sings? Does he throw his head back or flutter his wings? That's all stuff you want to observe and put on your announcement." We began to move closer to the sparrow, but it flew off. Budney explained to Christin that savannah sparrows like to call from favorite perches and this bird would likely return if we just waited quietly. We moved to within forty feet of the perch, then settled onto the ground, making ourselves as inconspicuous as possible. After five minutes, the sparrow returned, landing on sage, not the perch he'd used moments ago. He sang for a few minutes, a dry, buzzy, raspy song, then moved to another perch, closer, and sang again. He appeared nervous, though, concerned with our presence. Budney suggested that all of us except Christin should stand up slowly and leave. "Birds can't count," he said. This was an old trick that sometimes works. The bird is fooled into thinking the disturbing creatures have left. As we prepared to leave, Christin wondered aloud if she should wait to start the tape recorder until the bird got close. "Don't wait," Budney said. "Record him when he sings again even if he's not as close as you want. Tape is the cheapest part of your system. Just roll tape."

All the workshop leaders were spending this first morning with those who had the least experience with recording equipment and birds. For a beginner, knowing how to carry the tape recorder so cables didn't become entangled was a challenge, and the degree of difficulty was increased if one had to step over a barbwire fence with a parabolic mike. Beyond practical concerns was a more complex problem—knowing what type of recording equipment was best for a particular purpose, environment, and subject. This depended on understanding the physics of sound.

When the meadowlark Eduardo recorded sang from his perch, the breath he expelled displaced air molecules the same way a pebble tossed into a lake displaces water. The meadowlark's song rippled outward through the cold morning air as sound waves traveling roughly eleven hundred feet per second. When the waves reached Eduardo's microphone, the physical energy was transformed by the microphone into analogous variations in electrical current sent via cable to the tape recorder. The Nagra amplified the electrical signal, then directed it to the recording head, a small electromagnet. Electrical current passing into an electromagnet produces a magnetic field. Because tape is coated with iron oxide (or some other magnetically sensitive material), the magnetic field affects the alignment of iron particles inside a film on the polyester tape. Particles are polarized, as if each is a tiny bar magnet. The distinctive pattern of the particles reflects the variations in the magnetic field, which are a reflection of variations in the electrical current. Those variations, in turn, reflect the varied pressure of the sound waves—the meadowlark's song.

This is an ideal picture of the process, unlikely to exist even in the controlled environment of a sound studio, to say nothing of a marsh in California where the variables range from wind disrupting the sound waves to batteries losing energy. Eduardo's meadowlark was more than a hundred feet away. By the time the sound waves reached the microphone, they had dissipated considerably just as ripples in the water eventually smooth out. Thus, Budney's dictum: halve the distance, double the gain.

The microphone and recorder, of course, affect the recording quality, as does the tape itself. Good tape recorders can be adjusted to match the tape. Chromium oxide tapes, for example, produce better magnetization than iron oxide tapes, but they require a different bias, the high-frequency signal the recorder adds to the sound signal to enhance polarization of the magnetized particles. Without bias, more particles remain unpolarized. Particles that remain random produce tape hiss. The tape in Eduardo's Nagra was one-quarter inch wide compared to one-eighth-inch tape used in cassettes. The wider the tape the more particles to store information, thus the finer the resolution. In addition, the faster tape travels across the recording head the more particles are used to represent each moment of sound recorded. This is one of the advantages of reel-to-reel recorders. Their tape speed is generally fifteen or seven and a half inches per second, compared to one and seven-eighths inches per second in cassette tapes. Always there are trade-offs. A standard five-inch reel of tape traveling at fifteen inches per second will allow only eight minutes of recording time compared to sixty minutes for cassette tapes.

There were dozens more elements to consider. Digital recorders are lighter and produce no tape hiss. But they are power hogs, going through rechargeable nickel-cadmium power packs in ninety minutes; the D cell batteries in a Nagra last for twenty-five hours. Budney doled out this information throughout the week. To the least experienced recordists at the workshop, recording birdsong must have seemed like trying to catch a snowflake. Budney and the others patiently offered advice and encouragement at (sometimes literally) every step. The future of bioacoustics, a science still in its infancy, depended on people like Eduardo and Christin. It depended as well on recordists with no scientific agenda, people who simply recorded for the challenge and the pleasure of spending early mornings listening to the world wake up. Rich Peet, one of the recordists, had brought his thirty-six-inch parabola with him, as large a dish as anyone is likely to carry. It looked imposing, difficult to handle, but Rich extolled its virtues when people gathered near the vans for breakfast. One could record a bird a hundred, even two hundred feet away. Rich's parabola was covered with a furry cloth, wrapped over the open dish like plastic wrap over a bowl of food. This was a windshield, and though windshields for a large parabola can be expensive, Rich had made his own covering, using fake fur from a fabric store. "It only cost six dollars a yard," he said. Last night when people were introducing themselves, there were several audible gasps when Rich said he had quit his job a few weeks earlier so he could record birds through the bird-song season. "I promised my wife I'd get another job when the summer was over," he said.

No one else had gone to such extremes, but people commonly used vacation time for recording trips. Dave Herr, who works for the National Forest Service, takes vacation days to help Budney conduct the workshop. Neither he nor Randy Little are paid. Greg Clark, a former workshop participant who owns a business in Arizona, came to the workshop this year for technical support. Clark brought a new computer to burn a compact disc of each participant's best recording at the end of the week. In fact, he arrived early and spent the first couple of days crawling in the dining hall attic to rewire the building's electrical connections. Each year Budney had lamented the lack of enough outlets to plug in all the equipment, but no more: shiny new electrical boxes were now positioned throughout the room.

When people were finished with breakfast and headed out for another hour of recording, Budney watched as Eduardo walked down the road. Eduardo's presence at the workshop was part of Ted Parker's legacy. Wally Shriner, Eduardo's professor at Mount Hood Community College, took the workshop a couple of years ago. When two people canceled their enrollment this year, Budney called Shriner and asked if he had any promising students who would benefit from the experience. Eduardo was perfect for it, and Budney couldn't have been happier. The college paid Eduardo's airfare. LNS waived all fees and was paying his room and board at the field station as part of an ongoing program for Latin American students funded by donations made to LNS in Ted Parker's memory. Parker had always worked closely with local people in South America, recognizing that the fate of the New World tropics depended greatly on local involvement in conservation programs. As Budney lingered for a moment by the vans, he motioned toward Eduardo walking down the road: "One guy like that in Panama can do a lot of good things."

On the second full day of the workshop we headed north into the mountains to Bear Trap Meadow, a small, beautiful valley whose slopes were covered with lodgepole pines and red firs. The meadow ran east-west for a few hundred yards, and a stream—edged in places with clumps of short, shrubby alders—wandered through it. One of the advantages of holding the workshop in the Sierra Nevada was being able to go from a freshwater marsh in the Sierra Valley one day to an alpine meadow the next. The birds were different and the challenges the environment presented for recordings were different. The wide-open sight lines afforded by the marsh the day before were now just a pleasant memory. Bear Trap was filled with obstacles, and the running water of the stream, pretty as it was, was undesirable background noise if one wanted to record a bird's song. When we arrived, daylight had spilled into the area and birds were already singing, though the sun would not rise over the ridge to the east for some time yet. This morning no one waited for instructions. People gathered their gear and headed off in different directions. Yesterday, Budney had reminded everyone of field-recording etiquette: walk slowly and quietly, point one's microphone at the ground when not recording, be careful not to walk into someone else's recording field, and if it was necessary to talk, whisper.

I stood for a moment on the edge of the road that came in along the western slope. Two or three people remained on the slope, but most had headed into the meadow below, slowly spreading out through the valley. It was a strange and beautiful scene. Figures were moving through the wet grass of the meadow in slow motion like browsing deer. They stepped cautiously or stood in one spot, leaving their feet planted and turning at the waist if they heard a bird to one side. Or they bent low and twisted their heads to find the best recording angle. One would slowly raise an arm with a microphone straight out toward the sound and freeze in position. Another held a parabolic mike and swept the horizon with it at the speed of a drifting cloud. Someone else stood unmoving with head bowed, inspecting some dial or switch. From my perspective on the slope above, it looked like tai chi with tape recorders, high-tech pantomime with mittens and Polarfleece.

This was the pace and the sound of the world at rest. And a chance to slow down and hear only the sounds of birds and wind in the trees and water flowing over rocks was an unspoken benefit of the workshop. I remembered the first time I'd accompanied Budney on a recording trip. It was 1995, and we were camped in the coastal mountains of Oregon. One evening he set up a stereo microphone on the forest floor of needles and moss and laid out a hundred feet of cable so he could operate the recorder from a distance. He left the microphone and cable in place, then we retired to our tents for the evening. We were in an area known locally as the Valley of the Giants, a 350-acre remnant of ancient Douglas fir that had been spared the clear-cutting that had denuded much of the landscape in these mountains. At 3 A.M. I got up. I sat for a moment in the small opening among the centuries-old Douglas fir, trying to clear my head. Above me I could see the brushstroke of the Milky Way, and the odd, steadily gleaming sphere of a satellite moving clocklike across the heavens.

Moments later Budney emerged from his tent, sleepy-eyed. He splashed water on his face, picked up his tape recorder and flashlight, and headed down the logging road. Before long he turned into the forest, waving his flashlight about to pick out a trail of orange surveyor's tape tied to the branches of understory trees. I followed him, stumbling up a slope. When Budney found the cable, he connected it to the recorder, then followed the cable to the microphone and inspected it to see that it was dry and clean. Retracing his footsteps, Budney sat down next to the recorder. I settled down on a plush bed of needles and moss and leaned back against the massive trunk of a Douglas fir, getting as comfortable as possible. Once Budney turned on the recorder, he didn't want any movements that would create noise. Though we were a hundred feet away from the microphone, it was sensitive enough to pick up the sound of twigs crunching underneath us or the rustling of clothing.

Budney turned on the tape recorder and we sat quietly. What he hoped to get on tape—from the predawn darkness through first light of day and into the early morning—was "what an old-growth forest sounds like." When he'd told me that the day before, I'd stared blankly at him for a second. I hadn't thought of a forest as having a sound of its own, as if it were a single living organism. But this is how Budney thinks of the world, as a collection of sounds. Sometimes he listens for individual notes—the *pip* call of an olive-sided flycatcher, for instance—and at other moments he takes in the whole symphony of vibrations that stirs the air around him. It was something I could appreciate as we sat there in the dark forest. We were far enough away from any city lights that when I reached out my hand, it began to disappear in the darkness. My eyes were useless, but I could smell the forest, I could feel it, and I could hear it. The stillness itself seemed palpable, a slight pressure around the body that was released moments later when the first call notes of a Pacific-slope flycatcher pricked the silence—*suwhit, suwhit*. Then a winter wren began his exuberant aria, one of the longest and most complex bird songs known. Moments later, a varied thrush began to sing. In the deep wells of silence between the immense Douglas firs, the bird songs seemed small, as quick and sharp as flashes of light from a jewel in the sun.

Budney removed the headphones he was using to monitor what he was recording and handed them to me. When I put them on, I felt as if I had dived to the bottom of a lake. I was no longer aware of anything except what I heard, and I heard much more than I had a few seconds ago. Somewhere, something was rustling in the leaf litter, a mouse perhaps. A twig snapped, and high above me a light breeze whispered through the crowns of the firs. The flycatcher's call was louder and clearer. The wren's song was symphonic. Then, suddenly, I felt—not heard, but felt—a low, hollow drumming reverberating in the headphones, as if a moth were fluttering its wings against my ears. I mouthed the word *grouse* to Budney and gave him a quizzical look. I couldn't think of what else it could be. It was not the first time I had heard the drumming sound that grouse make by flapping their wings rapidly, but this was different. I felt each ripple. Never had I been so aware that sounds are vibrations in the air—the air compressed hundreds or thousands of times per second by whatever force sets it in motion.

The drumming faded away. I gave the headphones back to Budney, and we sat quietly, listening to the flycatcher, wren, and thrush. They were the only sounds we heard. Budney was hoping to hear nothing but forest sounds for at least a couple of hours before man-made noises intruded. Although we were in the middle of the largest remaining tract of old-growth forest in Oregon's coastal mountains and it was still an hour before sunrise, we were not out of range of the sounds of people going about their lives. Today, though, was Memorial Day. Holidays and weekends are good for recording. Budney knew that people would be getting up later than usual, and fewer people would be going to work. Thus, fewer engines would start up this morning. Budney's sensitive microphone would pick up even a distant engine and lay its sound onto the tape like a film of dust on a clean window, ruining the otherwise natural soundscape. Airplanes flying overhead—holiday or no—would create a rumbling hum that would nearly drown out the sounds of birds only a few yards away.

Earlier Budney had excitedly spoken of possibly getting a definitive recording of old-growth forest, a "sound portrait" of the habitat. "It's just like a photographic document," Budney said, "except that it's really more lifelike. Photographs reduce three dimensions to two, but a good recording loses virtually nothing." The day before, when Budney had said he wanted a recording of what an old-growth forest sounded like, he added, "just in case," which reminded me that in the Library of Natural Sound's collection is the only known recording of the call of the ivory-billed woodpecker, now thought to be extinct (though there have been sporadic reports in recent years, some of particular interest in Louisiana). In 1935, Arthur A. Allen and Peter Paul Kellogg, the library's founders, spent six months driving around the eastern United States in a truck with several hundred pounds of equipment to record "the voices of vanishing species of birds," as Kellogg later wrote. Sound recording was new, and one of the best methods available at the time to record sound was on 35mm motion-picture film, so a visual record of the ivory-billed woodpecker exists as well. One evening, in his house outside Ithaca, Budney showed me the film footage Allen and Kellogg had gotten of the ivory-bill. When one of the birds, clinging to the trunk of a tree, turned its head and called, it was the bird's voice, not its image, that was haunting. I heard the ivory-bill's short, single note (resembling "the false, high note of a clarionet [*sic*]," John James Audubon wrote) much as Allen and Kellogg had, as if the bird were still calling more than half a century later for anyone who might be listening.

Disappearing more quickly and completely than any endangered species or ecosystem are places—forests, seashores, deserts, plains, mountains—where we might stop and listen to the world and hear only natural sounds. Budney has recorded birds throughout North America, and in South America, Africa, and Antarctica, and nearly everywhere he's been his microphone picks up man-made noises. Gordon Hempton, a friend of Budney's and an Emmy-winning natural-sound recordist and self-proclaimed "acoustic ecologist," found twenty-one sites in the state of Washington in 1984 where he could record for at least fifteen minutes without man-made noise intruding on the soundscape. In 2000, that was true of only three of the sites. Several years ago, Hempton launched the One Square Inch of Silence campaign, in which he asked that the National Park Service designate one square inch of a national park as a zone dedicated to only natural sounds. Hempton's sly logic gets at the heart of the problem. One square inch of silence would require a large noise-free zone surrounding it. Noise is invasive. One cannot look away from an unpleasant sound. A chain saw far from view rattles in the ears of someone walking on an otherwise peaceful trail. In the cities and suburbs, the beat from a stereo penetrates a neighbor's walls and becomes his beat. We make temporary retreats to national forests and so-called wilderness areas in large part to escape the din of our mechanized, commerce-infested lives. Most of us live smack in the middle of the auditory equivalent of a county dump.

No one has put it better than writer Mark Slouka: "Ensnared in webs of sound, those of us living in the industrialized West today must pick our way through a discordant, infinite-channeled auditory landscape. Like a radio stuck on permanent scan, the culture lashes us with skittering bits and bytes, each dragging its piece of historical or emotional context: a commercial overheard in traffic, a falsely urgent weather report, a burst of canned laughter, half a refrain. The pager interrupts lectures, sermons, second acts, and funerals. Everywhere a new song begins before the last one ends, as though to guard us against even the potential of silence. Each place we turn, a new world—synthetic, fragmented, often as not jacked into the increasingly complex grid that makes up the global communications network—encroaches on the old world of direct experience, of authentic, unadorned events with their particular, unadorned sounds."

While many people would recognize Slouka's description and feel that it speaks for them, others would ridicule the sentiment. If noise is sound that is "loud, unpleasant, unexpected, or undesired," as the *American Heritage Dictionary* puts it (the word comes from the same Latin root as for *nausea*), then it follows of course that one person's undesirable noise is another's source of pleasure or simply unnoticed by-product of his actions. As many people are unconcerned with the effects of an increasingly noisy world as there are people undisturbed that the ivory-billed woodpecker will not pass this way again. Values are involved, as are individual personalities. I remember, though, the words of ornithologist John Fitzpatrick, director of Cornell's Lab of Ornithology, in response to the pro-developers' outcry that environmentalists want to save everything. "No, we don't," Fitzpatrick said. "All we want to do is save the few crumbs of the pie that are left so we can smell them and imagine what the whole pie was like."

One can question the definition of "natural sounds." Why is a woodpecker's "hammering" on a tree as it excavates a nest cavity any different from the hammering I hear coming from the new subdivision two blocks away? Perhaps it comes down to what is mechanized and what isn't. Once we created machines to do what had once been done by hand or could not be done at all, the nature of the sounds our species creates changed forever. An individual driving a nail into a two-by-four sounds different from the repetitive, explosive thuds of a nail gun. Leaf blowers and brooms couldn't be more dissimilar in their sound effects. A chorus of voices raised to song or the most energetic drum-playing does not compare to sound that is electronically amplified. It's true as well that nearly all of the sounds of the "discordant, infinite-channeled auditory landscape" most of us live in are in one way or another the sounds of buying and selling. Whether one is troubled by it or not, studies indicate it is taking a toll on our mental and physical health. High blood pressure, heart disease, headaches, insomnia, and gastrointestinal disorders have all been linked to noise. A report published in the *Journal of the American Medical Association* observed that nearly 15 percent of young people between the ages of six and nineteen showed signs of hearing loss. A National Health Interview Survey found that hearing problems in the forty-six-to-sixty-four-year age group had risen 26 percent between 1971 and 1990. And how else to explain the $100 million per year sales (by one estimate) of nature sound recordings—if we can't have the sound of the natural world *in* the natural world, we can bring it inside with us and play it loud enough to drown out the noise of the neighbor's television.

Standing above Bear Trap Meadow, far from the hurly-burly of the civilized world, I remembered that only four days earlier I had hustled through the Reno airport, the sound of the whistles and bells of the slot machines bouncing off the walls. It made the absence of such noise there in the mountains all the more luxurious. I couldn't help but wonder what it would be like if all our days contained only natural sounds. Would we listen once again to the wind and know what it meant? Would we hear as much as we see? There is, of course, no way to know—we closed that door behind us long ago—but listening to a bird singing touches something in our ancient past. Birdsong is like light streaming through the key-hole from a lost world.

Bear Trap Meadow was not a lost world, but it was wonderfully quiet and peaceful, and this morning it seemed remote and cut off from the paved, electric world, though we were not far from the highway and field station. The meadow, shaped like a bowl, which kept noise out and natural sound in, seemed to have a lucid stillness that one could almost touch. It was particularly cold this morning, thirty-two degrees when we left the station, and breaths full of frigid air only made the valley seem more pure. At 6 A.M. the sun rose over the eastern ridge and illuminated the dewy grasses of the meadow. It affected the birds like a second showing of first light. Flycatchers that had been shivering in the willows by the stream were now bathed in direct sunlight. A warbling vireo on the edge of the meadow began to sing. A chipping sparrow flew to the tip of a tall fir and let out his rapid trill. A red-breasted nuthatch called from somewhere up the slope, and high in another fir a western tanager sang.

The finest birdsong of the morning, though, was not quite a song. Some birds are better instrumentalists than vocalists. Susannah Buhrman had discovered a red-breasted sapsucker who was drumming on a metal trail-marker sign. The sound of his drumming rang in the cold mountain air, reverberating off the trunks of trees. The resonance and tone the sapsucker was getting from the metal triangle would have made any percussionist happy. Furthermore, the sapsucker wasn't just hammering steadily. The cadence varied. It was slow, then fast, then slow again, and ended with two final rapid taps. It was a sound to rival the vocal song of any songbird. I have heard the drumming of woodpeckers all my life and am sometimes awakened in the morning by a red-bellied woodpecker delivering a drumroll on the side of the house, but I had never heard anything quite like this. This sound was deep and rich.

Woodpeckers are known to use man-made objects that resonate to their liking. And for some species (yellow-bellied sapsucker, northern flicker, downy woodpecker, hairy woodpecker among them) drumming serves the same function as song. In some cases, male and female woodpeckers engage in ritualistic drumming at a possible nest site, as if to examine the musical potential of the tree. This red-breasted sapsucker had found a man-made instrument in a natural amphitheater. He returned all morning to the trail marker. I circled back to the spot several times to listen to him. At one point, I stood with Frank Dorritie, who had come to record the sapsucker. Frank, head of the Recording Arts Department at Los Medanos College in California, listened to the sapsucker for several minutes until it flew off again. "He's playing the opening notes to 'Dueling Banjos,'" Frank said. The comment surprised me. I had been too absorbed in the woodpecker's drumming to think of anything else, but Frank was right. The sapsucker's succession of drummed notes with their pauses and shifts in speed sounded just like the first few notes of "Dueling Banjos" (a tune made famous in the movie *Deliverance*). Frank was making the kind of connection between the music of birds and man that has been made for centuries. Sometimes it involves a particular bird and set of notes. At other times it is more general–an instinctive recognition that we share something special with songbirds. The question we might have asked was whether we should be comparing the sapsucker's drumming to the music or the music to the sapsucker's drumming.

W hich came first, birdsong or human music? Among the figures in the famous Lascaux cave paintings, thought to be created around 14,000 BC, are a bird and a bird-headed man. Both are shown with their beaks open, as if calling. The bird-headed man may be letting out a cry of distress since he is falling backward under the hooves of a charging bison wounded by a spear still hanging from its flank. But what sound is coming from the bird perched on a post nearby? Is it also giving a distress call? Is it invoking some magical powers to save the man? Or is it singing a melody whose beauty intensifies the bloody drama? The answer, I suppose, is less important than the question, which recognizes that some kind of relationship exists; why else would the artist have rendered the man and bird with beaks open? Ancient art and poetry abound with references to singing birds. The Sumerian Tilmun myth, one of the earliest surviving works of literature, refers to bird vocalizations, and the oldest secular English music, "Sumer Is Icumen In," welcomes summer with the cuckoo's song. A list of such examples would go on for pages, as would a list of birdsong that appears in ritual and religion. In ancient Greece, soothsayers built special observation towers to watch and listen for birds because they believed that when birds called or sang, the gods were speaking. Our word *augury* means literally "bird talk."

Exactly how ancient our connection to birdsong is and how birdsong and music were first intertwined has long intrigued scientists and musicians. The origins of music may be lost in prehistory, but we have concrete evidence that our Paleolithic ancestors were playing music long ago. In 1995, archaeologists working a cave site in the mountains of western Slovenia uncovered part of a bear's thighbone shaped like a flute. The bone held remnants of four evenly spaced holes. Its structure was similar to other "bone flutes" discovered in Europe, but this artifact, estimated to be forty-four-thousand years old, predated the others. In February of 2000, a replica was played at an American Association for the Advancement of Science symposium in Washington, D.C. The sophisticated design of the bone flutes that have been discovered leads many to believe that humans have been creating musical instruments for hundreds of thousands of years. Jelle Atema, who played the replica of the forty-four-thousand-year-old flute, speculates that flutelike instruments may have resulted when people noticed that wind blowing over hollow objects created a pleasing sound. The first flutes were likely made from reeds or hollow sticks, though they of course would decompose and leave no trace. If music "is as ancient as some believe," writes Patricia Gray and her coauthors in a paper related to the 2000 conference, "this could explain why we find so much meaning and emotion in music even though we cannot explain why it makes us feel the way it does. Such an impenetrable vagueness about this most basic of human creations seems to signal that the roots of music lie closer to our ancient lizard brain than to our more recent reasoning cortex, that music has a more ancient origin even than human language."

Gray was also interested in the tones of the bone flutes. "What you immediately hear," she has said, "is the beauty of their sound. They make pure and rather haunting sounds in very specific scales. It didn't have to be this way. They could have sounded like duck calls." Given that they are closer to the tones of songbirds, it is not hard to imagine that early musicians were influenced by birdsong. Although this too is speculation, we can at least be fairly certain our ancestors heard many of the same songbirds we hear today. Birds began to evolve from reptiles around 150 million years ago, during the late Jurassic period. Roughly 60 million years ago, the modern orders of birds first diverged from their common ancestors. By the end of the Miocene, 5 million years ago, many modern genera of songbirds had formed. The individual species of songbirds as we now know them appear to have developed during the Pleistocene. Fossil evidence cannot tell us how songbirds behaved at the time or what they sounded like, but we can be fairly certain that when our ancestors began to communicate vocally, estimated at a half million years ago, the world was already filled with birdsong.

Gray and her colleagues (Gray is a professional keyboardist and artistic director of the National Musical Arts, ensemble-in-residence at the National Academy of Sciences) also tackle the question of whether birdsong can truly be considered music, an issue that has preoccupied many ornithologists and musicians. William Thorpe addressed the matter in the first chapter of the first book on birdsong studies. Thorpe's *Bird-Song,* published in 1961, is primarily an account of his experiments with the chaffinch, but before he describes his chaffinch experiments, he asks why we call birdsong *song.* Thorpe applies several definitions of music to birdsong, all of which make more sense than not, though finally he is not satisfied with his own ruminations, especially when it comes to "the final criterion for artistic activity, namely the desire or intention to express or create something of beauty or significance [which with regards to birds] must remain in doubt." For some time, each new book on avian bioacoustics included a discussion of birdsong as music. In Charles Hartshorne's *Born to Sing,* published in 1973, the musicality of birdsong is a major theme. Hartshorne, in fact, rates birds worldwide for their singing accomplishments. Biologists, musicologists, psychologists, and others continue to examine the similarities between birdsong and music without coming to any firm conclusions. They stumble in part because defining music itself is problematic, made more so, Patricia Gray notes, by the work of such postmodernist composers as John Cage, whose famous convention-defying composition "4' 33''" calls for exactly four minutes and thirty-three seconds of "silence" to be performed by any instrument or combination of instruments.

If it is impossible to make an irrefutable case for birdsong as music by way of definitions and analysis, perhaps we should trust our instincts as have many of our greatest composers. Beethoven's Sixth Symphony includes passages that imitate the cuckoo, nightingale, and quail. Bartók's Piano Concerto no. 3 appears to include music inspired by birds he listened to on a visit to North Carolina, where he transcribed bird songs he first heard in the mountains. Some composers have been more direct in their treatment of bird songs: Messiaen's seven books of *Le Catalogue d'oiseaux* is based on remembered and annotated birdsong; performances of Respighi's *Pines of Rome* include playing a phonograph recording of a real nightingale; and American composer James Fassett has written *Symphony of Birds,* consisting entirely of songs and calls of real birds.

Then there was Mozart's pet starling. Among Mozart's compositions is an odd piece known as *A Musical Joke* for its discordant sounds. For centuries musicians have dressed in costumes to play the composition, thought to caricature the popular music of Mozart's day. One record jacket described the music this way: "In the first movement we hear the awkward, unproportioned, and illogical piecing together of uninspired material . . . [later] the andante cantabile contains a grotesque cadenza which goes on far too long and pretentiously and ends with a comical deep pizzicato note . . . and by the concluding presto, our 'amateur composer' has lost all control of his incongruous mixture."

Meredith West and Andrew King, psychologists interested in learning behavior and birds, understand the musical joke differently. In a 1990 paper, they lay out a careful case that links Mozart's composition with the vocalizations of a starling he kept for several years. West and King begin their paper by analyzing the vocalizations of starlings—among the best mimics in the bird world. They note that starlings raised as pets develop a striking repertoire that mixes human sounds with typical starling vocalizations. The starlings they write about sang "rambling tunes composed of songs originally sung or whistled to them intermingled with whistles of unknown origin and starling sounds." And "the tendency to sing off-key and to fracture the phrasing of the music at unexpected points" was common. One bird sang "a fragment of 'The Star-Spangled Banner' with frequent interpositions of squeaking noises," and another "routinely linked the energetically paced *William Tell* Overture to 'Rockaby Baby.'" The birds also sometimes repeated phrases in odd situations. One bird repeated "'basic research' as he struggled frantically with his head caught in string; another screeched, 'I have a question!' as she squirmed while being held to have her feet treated for an infection."

From this description of starling mimicry, West and King proceed to some detective work on Mozart's composition. Mozart purchased his starling on May 27, 1784. He recorded the purchase in a diary of expenses he kept. In the same entry he transcribed a melody he heard the starling whistle. West and King speculate that the melody may be what attracted Mozart to the bird in the first place. The transcribed tune (which Mozart accompanied with an admiring comment) closely resembled a theme that occurs in the final movement of Mozart's Piano Concerto in G Major, a work he had completed only the month before. How could the bird have known the music? Mozart had taken great pains to keep the composition secret until it was completed. Perhaps, West and King suggest, he had visited the market on other occasions while he was working on the concerto and absentmindedly whistled what he was composing, as was his habit. If so, the starling might have picked it up (starlings need hear something only once in order to mimic it perfectly) and then happened to repeat it when Mozart returned. Some have suggested a more tantalizing explanation: Mozart heard the starling's tune and worked it into his composition. West and King doubt this, but in either case, Mozart clearly grew fond of his starling and was apparently grief-stricken when it died three years later. He wrote a poem for the starling and arranged an elaborate burial ceremony for it. He insisted his friends attend in proper funeral attire. The veiled mourners marched in a procession and sang hymns. Mozart recited the poem at the bird's graveside.

West and King point to this as proof that the starling was not an ignored household pet. Mozart was likely intrigued by a bird with such powers of mimicry, and he almost certainly knew the bird's vocalizations and singing behavior well. Thus, it seems more than coincidence that the first composition Mozart completed after the starling died was *A Musical Joke*. The composition, West and King note, bears "the vocal autograph of a starling. . . . The 'illogical piecing together' is in keeping with the starlings' intertwining of whistled tunes. The 'awkwardness' could be due to the starlings' tendencies to whistle off-key or to fracture musical phrases at unexpected points. The presence of drawn-out, wandering phrases of uncertain structure also is characteristic of starling soliloquies. Finally, the abrupt end, as if the instruments had simply ceased to work, has the signature of starlings written all over it."

At dinner after our day at Bear Trap Meadow, Budney stood up and announced the plans for the next day. "We're going to Carman Valley," he said. "You are going to get a chance to hear something that even most experienced bird-watchers never hear—the predawn song of the gray flycatcher. They sing from a perch and usually don't move, so you'll be able to get a good recording. They sing this song only for a while before and during first light, so this is really a great opportunity." Budney continued to talk enthusiastically about the gray flycatcher's song, then noted that it took about forty minutes to get to Carman Valley and the flycatcher only sang his predawn song for a short while. "We'll leave at three-forty-five tomorrow," he said. Those who were still finishing their desserts stopped eating. Several people groaned. Budney stopped his speech as people began to talk.

"Could some of us leave with a later van, if we're not interested in recording the flycatcher?" someone asked.

Budney hemmed and hawed, then took a new approach. "Maybe Don Kroodsma will point out the predawn song of the chipping sparrow too. That's another song that few people hear."

Kroodsma had arrived at lunchtime, and Budney introduced him as one of the top experts on birdsong, but

Kroodsma downplayed this. "I'm just a tourist here," he said. And moments later he slipped away from the workroom and spent most of the afternoon setting up his tent and taking a nap. Now, sitting near the back of the dining hall, Kroodsma spoke up loudly: "I think I want to leave earlier than that." Several people smiled, assuming Kroodsma was joking. "I'm going to leave around three-fifteen," Kroodsma said. "I think three-forty-five is too late."

The hall was quiet for several seconds. Kroodsma said nothing else. Smiles turned to quizzical looks. Budney, still standing, spoke again: "I guess we could take some people in a later van. How many people would want to do that?" Two or three hands went up, then dropped. A short while later, as several people took out their tape recorders to review the day's recordings, Kroodsma asked Budney for directions to Carman Valley, then left the dining hall and walked to his tent.

At four-thirty the next morning, under a full moon obscured by drifting clouds, we arrived at Carman Valley. As people stepped out of the vans, Budney heard a gray flycatcher calling nearby. "There's the first song," he said. "We'll have to hurry. Follow that song." We could hear two other flycatchers in the near distance, so the group divided up. The call was two simple notes—*chi-bit*—which the bird repeated over and over rapidly. Within minutes, everyone disappeared into the darkness and I lost track of Budney. I walked toward the song of a flycatcher and stopped beneath the tree it was coming from. *Chi-bit, chi-bit, chi-bit.* Over and over the bird sang the two plain notes.

The gray flycatcher is as nondescript as the name suggests and is one of the notoriously difficult-to-identify *Empidonax* flycatchers. Flycatchers in the *Empidonax* genus are nearly identical in appearance. Because each species prefers a different habitat, one can rely on this as a clue, but their unique vocalizations are the surest indicators. In the predawn darkness at

Carman Valley, vocalization was the only indicator. With the moon hidden by clouds, first light still half an hour away, I could see no more than a couple of feet. For twenty minutes I listened to the flycatcher sing—*chi-bit, chi-bit, chi-bit, chi-bit, chi-bit, chi-bit*—and just as first light began to show, the bird slowed his song. He paused longer between each *chi-bit,* as if running out of energy. Although the song was plain, the performance was impressive. As the darkness lifted and I could see the tree in front of me, I discovered I wasn't alone. Five other people were standing quietly around the tree like background props on a stage. Keeping their microphones pointed skyward, they looked down to check their VU meters now that they could see them. And then, within moments, some kind of internal spring in the flycatcher wound down until a minute or two went by between *chi-bit*s. Finally there was a long silence.

The flycatcher would call on and off throughout the day, but this predawn ritual was over. Those who had been recording the flycatcher headed off silently in different directions. I wandered down the access road toward the call of a red-breasted nuthatch. His nasal twang fell just short of a musical tone, as if the bird were playing "a paper trumpet," as the poet W. S. Merwin has observed. I remembered that Merwin's nuthatch was a different species on another continent in a "distant morning" (the title of the poem), and perhaps because this came to mind and the sound echoed among the pines under an overcast sky, the nuthatch's call sounded a bit lonely. I followed the nuthatch until he stopped calling, then doubled back toward a birdsong I could not identify, but it slipped away before I could grasp its pattern.

Three hours later, when we gathered at the vans for breakfast, Kroodsma wandered in. He had left the station half an hour before everyone else this morning, as he said he would, and though we passed his car beside the road as we entered Carman Valley, he was already somewhere in the darkness waiting for a flycatcher to sing his first notes. Now he stood off to the side of the group. Kroodsma has the fair complexion and blue eyes of his Dutch ancestors, and something about his handsome, square-jawed face—an openness and brightness— puts one at ease. At the moment, though, he seemed shy. People milled about, eating their cereal and bagels. Budney turned toward Kroodsma and asked, loud enough for all to hear, "Don, what can you tell us about this dawn chorus? And about the gray flycatcher? Or maybe the chipping sparrow? They have a predawn song too, don't they?"

Kroodsma took a moment to respond. "Oh . . . what can I say? The experience is greater than the words I can muster to describe it. I just had to be out here this morning before the birds were singing. I needed to feel the world wake up, to feel the sunrise approaching one mile every five seconds and this dawn chorus sweeping towards me, just to feel that energy that these birds put into it. And then these gray flycatchers, they're singing at arm's reach. We could almost walk up to them and just grab them right out of the bush. There's just an extraordinary energy that happens in that last half hour before sunrise. So few people get out and appreciate it. What's going on here is largely a mystery, and maybe that's why it's so exciting. It's the mystery of what happens at dawn. Why all this singing at dawn? Oh, you could list ten different reasons why birds might sing at dawn, and there are some obvious ones—like it's quiet and the sound carries a long way, and maybe the bird wants to tell everyone that he's awake and alive and made it through the night. A lot of mortality occurs during the night. And you can think of other reasons—maybe it's too dark to do anything else, it's too dark to find food. So why not sing? But none of these reasons really explain it. You still have to know why the bird is singing, why he is putting all of this energy into song."

Kroodsma stopped a moment.

"Tell us about chipping sparrows," Budney said.

Kroodsma turned his face upward and closed his eyes for a moment. Some of the participants certainly were familiar with the chipping sparrow, one of the most common birds in North America. It has a distinctive appearance, a rust-red cap, sharp white line above the eye, and a black line through the eye, but a plain, seemingly dull song—a raspy trill of two or three seconds duration, usually delivered on one pitch.

"I have had a graduate student working with me for the last couple of years on the chipping sparrow," Kroodsma said, "and he has gone out every morning at four-thirty to a cemetery where chipping sparrows are common. He hasn't missed a morning unless he was sick, and that is the kind of persistence it takes to understand what's going on. This morning I listened to chipping sparrows right here. I was listening to one chipping sparrow over here and another one over there. And chipping sparrow songs are usually very different. The one over here had a very fast buzzy song, and the one over there was a drier rattle. You can tell most chipping sparrows apart by their individually distinctive songs. So you can even tell what they're doing in the dark when you can't see them."

Kroodsma described the cemetery near Amherst where he and his graduate student listened to chipping sparrows. In the spring when the male sparrows arrive from their wintering grounds to the south, the cemetery becomes a dense chipping sparrow neighborhood with twenty-five to thirty birds on carefully guarded territories. Walking at sunrise through the cemetery, Kroodsma can hear one bird after another singing, each with a slightly different song. Now and then, however, he comes across two males with identical songs.

"One of the questions we always ask," said Kroodsma, "is from whom does a bird learn its song. My student banded a lot of baby chipping sparrows and followed them everywhere. One bird might go a mile away during his hatching summer and settle next to a bachelor male who was singing nonstop. It was the perfect opportunity for this youngster, as he was fighting for his own little space, to learn this new neighbor's song. And we have lots of other examples like this where a young bird leaving home rejects his father's song and learns a new song at that new location. And that gives him an advantage for setting up a territory there. This is the song the sparrow sings for the rest of his life. If both birds return to the same territory the following spring, then they will share a song, but so many birds either die during the winter or settle on new territories the following spring that most neighboring chipping sparrows have different songs. If you listen a bit, you can tell one sparrow from another.

"At dawn and during the day they all have their territories, all spaced out, and they'll be singing from the middle of those territories. They are singing all around and their songs may be three seconds long. That is what most people hear. But there's something else going on too. In this magical time—when it's still dark out, before first light—several sparrows will gather in something like a chipping sparrow arena and sing these rapid-fire songs back and forth, one song every second with hardly a pause between them. They are like machine-gun bursts, sometimes overlapping each other, sometimes timed to alternate. For roughly half an hour, each bird sings as many as thirty songs per minute rather than the typical five or six it sings later in the morning. What can this mean?

"There is a dominance hierarchy that we can show. There is always one bird that starts singing first in this group. If you take him away, another bird steps forward. The best guess is that this hierarchy is negotiated during this brief time before dawn. You will not hear this unless you get up well before sunrise. You will not know it ever happened. And this negotiating may set the stage for what happens throughout the rest of the day. We don't know for sure."

Again, Kroodsma paused. "Are females listening?" he asked. "Our best guess is yes. It seems to be a display of singing prowess: Who can sing the fastest, who can sing the loudest? My graduate student had four birds in one little clump. He removed three of them and the fourth one didn't bother singing. So it's a matter of this social competition. What exactly is going on? We can only guess. My student took blood from all the babies from the nests in the neighborhood to see who was actually the father of the babies in the various nests. We humans have been looking at birds through puritanical eyes, thinking they are monogamous. If you look at the DNA of the nestlings in a lot of nests—of all kinds of species— you discover there are many of what we call *extrapair* matings. Females have choices in the breeding season. They are paired with a given male who will help raise their offspring, but the females that are paired to males low in the hierarchy may mate also with the dominant male next door. If she can improve the quality of her offspring by having the dominant male father some of them, she'll do that. But she'll also continue mating with her own partner because then he will feel more committed to helping raise the young.

"So in chipping sparrows, in our study, we would love to see the correlation between who is fathering the young in the various nests and who is singing in what fashion at dawn—who sings first, who sings fastest or longest. You know, you think about it—we were pretty hungry by eight o'clock this morning. These birds have been fasting all night long. It probably takes tremendous energy for them to do all this singing. And maybe what better time is there for females to demand some kind of show by the males on an empty stomach of how long they can go and who can sing the longest and loudest? So . . . my best guess about all this fuss at dawn? It has to be about the birds negotiating their relationships with each other."

Kroodsma stopped talking, searching for a way to end his

impromptu lecture. "You know, there's one more thing I could say. We were talking earlier about how when you first start listening to birds to identify them by song, you listen for the pattern of the species song, as if all the individuals of the species sound alike. But the more you listen, the more you start to hear all the little details, and the whole world opens up to you when you start to recognize these birds as different individuals. You think that someone just beginning can't contribute much, but it is amazing how much is not known, and as soon as you start to listen carefully, you pick out things, and then you go to the literature and you read all the accounts and the experts don't mention any of this."

Some of the participants must have thought Budney had scripted these concluding remarks. "Beginners can make a difference" was second only to "halve the distance, double the gain" among his most frequently repeated remarks. Many people seemed to be increasingly comfortable with their recording equipment, but identifying birds remained a challenge. Tamara Smyth, a musician with a good ear for sound but little experience with birds, sat at a table one evening making a list in a notebook of what she had recorded and where each recording began and ended. Amused at her notes, she read them aloud: "Unidentified bird number one, unidentified bird number two, unidentified bird number three. . . ." It was a moment I could appreciate. Some people were under the impression that I knew bird songs quite well because I was able to identify a song now and then. It is true that I have watched birds all my life, but I frequently struggle to identify even a song I've heard many times. Sometimes I think I suffer from the auditory equivalent of color blindness. At the workshop I had the utmost respect for those who were novices at both recording and birding, and it seemed little short of miraculous that they could focus attention on a bird's song and a VU meter simultaneously.

Kroodsma, in fact, had left out a couple of details in his chipping sparrow story. He had first heard the chipping sparrows singing their predawn songs when he was visiting his mother in Michigan in the summer of 1993. He'd gotten up in darkness and driven along the streets with his window rolled down, listening. What he didn't tell the workshop group was that when he'd heard the sparrows singing these speeded-up songs that morning, throwing them back and forth at each other, he was so overcome by the display that he forgot to turn on his tape recorder.

The next morning, Kroodsma again left for the recording site well ahead of the group, and the following day he left even earlier, rising at 2 A.M. to go to Sierra Valley. During the remainder of the week, he drifted in and out of workshop activities like a ghost, joining in conversation at meals, but otherwise keeping to himself. After dinner each evening, he retired early to his tent. I had expected him to take a more active role in the workshop, but perhaps his absence rather than his presence—rising early to record by himself—would be the example the young scientists would take home with them.

One day we drove to Jones Valley, which held a particularly pretty, undisturbed meadow, the pale green sedge awash in lavender wildflowers. A few savannah sparrows sang from perches in the sedge, coyotes howled in the distance, a Townsend's solitaire appeared briefly on the forested slope to the northwest, and in midmorning, hidden high in a pine, a western tanager sang spiritedly his tumbling, rough-edged, robinlike song—a "robin with a sore throat," as it is often described. (Earlier in the week, I had heard the sweeter voice of a black-headed grosbeak—"a robin with voice lessons.") The following day we went to Lincoln Valley. The meadow was covered with frost. When the sun finally warmed the air, we were driven out of the area by hordes of mosquitoes, but not before I watched a calliope hummingbird, the smallest bird in North America, perform its mating dance. Bathed in the sun's first rays, he drew a forty-foot-high *U* in the air at blinding speed, zooming up, then down, and up again—over and over as if practicing hummingbird penmanship. On the final day of the workshop we returned to Bear Trap Meadow and the red-breasted sapsucker. Throughout the week there were lectures in the afternoons on digital editing systems, sound meters, and microphones, as well as a demonstration of how to solder a cable to a cable connector.

Each evening as I walked to my tent I heard the hermit thrush singing from somewhere amongst the pines. Some evenings he seemed farther away, the song so faint—a few strains of music from a far room—that I almost didn't notice it. Perhaps, I thought, he was facing away from me when he sang. Later, I would remember that others have noticed the ventriloquial nature of the hermit thrush's song. Thoreau, who thought the song expressed "the immortal beauty and wildness of the woods," went looking for a hermit thrush he heard singing one April day in 1852: "I go in search of him. He sounds no nearer. On a low bough of a small maple near the brook in the swamp, he sits with ruffled feathers, singing more low or with less power, as it were ventriloquizing; for though I am scarcely more than a rod off, he seems farther off than ever."

I never saw the hermit thrush, though most evenings, before I got too close to the river sound, I stopped and listened for a few minutes. The song was long and slow, so long that, at first, not able to call to mind the pattern of a hermit thrush song, I thought he was singing three songs in a row until I talked to Kroodsma one afternoon and he imitated the song. *Oh, holy holy, -ah purity purity, -eeh sweetly sweetly* is how

Kroodsma transcribes it. The pauses between sections produce a tension between the momentary silence and the next note, an anticipation, almost as if the thrush knows how beautiful his song is and so teases the listener by seeming to stop in mid-melody. The notes shift in pitch up and down the scale (he is using both halves of his syrinx simultaneously), and the final notes fade a bit. It is as bittersweet as any sound I've heard. "It affects us as part of our unfallen selves," Thoreau wrote in his journal. Descriptions in bird books nearly always refer to the notes as "flutelike," "clear," and "ethereal," but I prefer bird expert Kenn Kaufman's word: "pensive." I imagine a bird who has realized, in the great silence of the forest at dusk, that he has been a hermit too long.

One evening late in the week, each person selected one or two recordings to play for the group. Susannah chose a recording of a yellow-headed blackbird because she'd taped the bird among a flock of vocalizing blackbirds, just the situation she would face in the fall when she attempted to record parrots in Bonaire. Rich Peet played his recording of the red-breasted sapsucker drumming on the trail marker. Christin had a good recording of the gray flycatcher, and another of two juncos. Eduardo's current favorite was a mountain quail. Among the other recordings were a snipe, Brewer's sparrow, pileated woodpecker, Cassin's finch, red-winged blackbird, and a hermit thrush. Nick Plava, the sound engineer from New York, played a recording of a rustling noise coming from the brush and then his own muffled exclamation—"Holy shit!"—when he finally saw the source of the sound that was coming closer and closer—a bear.

Although most of the participants prefaced their recording with self-deprecating remarks, and some had purposely chosen a recording with problems so they could get advice on how to improve their technique, many of the recordings were remarkably clear and sharp. When Santiago Imberti, a natural-history tour leader from Chile, played his cut of a pileated woodpecker, we heard first the bird's drumming, then a call. As soon as Budney heard the woodpecker's call, he shot a surprised look at Dave Herr: "Dave, have you ever gotten that call?" Herr, who has focused much of his recording on woodpeckers, made an exaggerated face of disappointment. "No," he said. "Not once."

It was a perfect example of what Budney had been preaching since the workshop began. One need not travel to exotic locations to get valuable recordings. Someone working in his own backyard could make a contribution. There were countless bird vocalizations that LNS did not yet have in the collection. "We don't have a good recording of a great horned owl from the Ithaca area," Budney told the group. The owls begin vocalizing in January and no one has yet spent enough time on winter nights in Ithaca to get a quality recording of the owl. Even beginners can make recordings that are useful, he insisted. And really, one never knew when a recording might be of use to someone else, so it was important to document your recordings and archive them somewhere. Preferably at LNS. Someone might come along later and find just what he needed in the recording you made.

Months later, I remembered Budney's comments when Kroodsma told me that for a project he was working on he had recently gone to LNS and listened to all the recordings of catbirds in the collection. One particular set of recordings had caught his attention. He'd looked at the notes on the tapes. They had been recorded by an amateur during his first week of recording birds. The notes read: "Recorded by Don Kroodsma, July 11, 1968, Pellston, Michigan."

III

III

From its beginnings in the 1950s, avian bioacoustics has focused on oscines, the "true songbirds." It is songbirds that learn their songs, and it is their great diversity in song and singing behavior that Kroodsma and others feel compelled to explain. Few studies exist on suboscines, the songbirds' closest relatives. Of these two suborders of the passerines, suboscines sing songs that are generally simple and unmusical and thus don't attract much attention. Once early research demonstrated that suboscines do not learn their vocalizations, the entire suborder was largely ignored. Because the vocalizations of suboscines are genetically encoded, there aren't many questions to answer nor any intriguing singing behaviors to attract a researcher. In general, suboscines have been studied only to show, by contrast, how special the oscines are.

In the 1980s Kroodsma was among those who conducted laboratory experiments on suboscines. He began by exposing young alder and willow flycatchers, two closely related species, to each other's song, but not their own. Both ignored the foreign vocalization and sang their own species song perfectly. Because he used taped songs broadcast on loudspeakers, he followed this by showing that eastern phoebes failed to imitate the vocalizations of live birds. Then, in a striking experiment, Kroodsma raised phoebes that had been deafened and discovered they still developed normal phoebe songs—arguably the most convincing evidence one could produce to show the songs were genetically encoded. Despite the results of his own studies, Kroodsma was troubled by the research on suboscines. Song development had been studied in fewer than a dozen species, and he wondered how representative they were of all suboscines. Researchers avoided the suboscines not only because there seemed to be little to learn from birds that displayed no song variation, but also because more than 95 percent of the roughly one thousand suboscine species are found in the tropics, and 90 percent of those in Central and South America. In North America, suboscines are represented by only a few species of flycatchers, but the neotropics have hundreds of species of flycatchers as well as antbirds, antwrens, woodcreepers, cotingas, and others belonging to the suborder.

"It's more convenient to work close to home," Kroodsma says. "The chickadee study is a perfect example. They are right there in my yard, and there's no end of interesting questions that can be asked about their songs." The uncertainties of fieldwork in tropical forests make for the greatest disincentive. In North America researchers take for granted a system of roads and trails to reach study sites, and they count on reliable sources of electricity for recharging batteries. Moreover, one can rely on an extensive network of biologists for basic information on birds in almost any area. When Kroodsma went to Nebraska to study the marsh wren, colleagues told him exactly where to go to find marsh wren communities. Far fewer biologists are working in the neotropics, and the language barrier adds to the difficulty. In addition to logistical problems, working in the humid tropics is tough on electronic equipment. For all these reasons, suboscines have received little attention—despite the promise they hold for shedding light on the mystery of mysteries: why learning evolved only in the oscines. If the question is ever to be answered, it will involve some kind of comparison between species in the two groups.

After Kroodsma published the results of his experiments with deafened phoebes in 1991, he began asking around about the singing behavior of suboscines in the tropics. When nothing came of his initial queries, he put his thoughts on suboscines aside and did more work on wrens. Then he got involved with the black-capped chickadee. In 1997, though, after a visit to LNS, his thoughts returned to suboscines. Before he left Ithaca, Kroodsma asked Greg Budney what he could listen to on the long drive back to Amherst. Budney gave him a copy of a newly produced compact disc of Costa Rican birds, and somewhere between Ithaca and Amherst—between the songs of trogons and white-throated robins—Kroodsma heard the song of the three-wattled bellbird. It sounded like nothing else on the CD. The song began with a loud *bonk*—bell-like, but perhaps a bell made of mahogany—and was followed by piercing whistles and some faint, barely audible swishing sounds. Kroodsma replayed the track and listened again. He was enthralled by the bellbird's strange vocalization, and hearing it brought back a conversation he'd had about suboscines with Gary Stiles, an expert on neotropical birds. Stiles, one of the people Kroodsma had contacted a few years earlier, had told him the bellbird's song varies from place to place. The three-wattled bellbird is a member of the cotinga family, a suboscine. Its song should be the same everywhere.

The following spring, Kroodsma made a trip to Costa Rica with two University of Massachusetts friends, Dave Stemple and Bruce Byers. He hoped to hear bellbirds at some point, but he had other birds in mind too. He intended to record birds on a wish list he had drawn up, primarily tropical birds known for the beauty and complexity of their songs. A Costa Rican ornithologist, Julio Sanchez, arranged for the group to stay in a cabin at Volcán Barva, a volcanic peak in Braulio Carrillo National Park in the central highlands. On their first morning, the four men rose before dawn and wandered off in different directions on the mountainside to record. Kroodsma went looking for slaty-backed nightingale-thrushes, but a couple of hours after sunrise he heard a three-wattled bellbird calling in the distance. "I just sort of dropped everything," Kroodsma says. "The bellbird was magnetic. Just amazing. I headed up the mountainside to get closer and record it." There was nothing musical about the song. It was about as far from the liquid melody of a slaty-backed nightingale-thrush as could be. The striking bell-like *bonk* rang out loudly, carrying down the mountainside louder than any other birdsong Kroodsma had ever heard. The whistles were almost shrill, and when Kroodsma trained his parabolic mike on the bird, he could hear softer sounds that were otherwise inaudible. They sounded like the swishing noise that comes from a churning washing machine.

Within minutes, all four men had gathered at the same spot to listen to the bellbird. Recording the vocalizations was difficult. The *bonk* was so loud and the swishing sounds so soft that Kroodsma had to turn the gain down on his recorder so the sound from the *bonk* wouldn't saturate the tape, then quickly turn it up to capture the swishing. The bellbird's appearance was as captivating as its vocalizations. It was a creature both beautiful and bizarre, something seemingly dreamed up by a birdmaker in an ambivalent mood. The size of a pigeon, the bellbird is a rich chestnut brown except for its head, neck, and upper chest, which are snow-white, as if the bird had been held by its feet and dipped in whitewash. From this white hood appear a black bill and black eyes encircled in more blackness as thick as gothic mascara. Most striking of all are the three long, black wattles that hang from the base of its bill like leeches. The wattles, normally two to three inches long, can be

extended to five inches, and to enthrall onlookers of the opposite sex, the bellbird may fling its wattles about like a fifteen-
year-old flipping her hair.

Kroodsma and the others recorded the bellbird for the
remainder of the morning, then walked back down the mountain to take a lunch break. Near the park headquarters they
ran into Debra Hamilton, another U.S. biologist. Hamilton
had arrived in Costa Rica in 1993 to do research for her master's degree and never left. Kroodsma struck up a conversation. What was she doing at Volcán Barva? he asked. Studying
bellbirds, she told him.

This was not the first time serendipity had played a role
in Kroodsma's research. Later he would compare the good
fortune of meeting Debra Hamilton on the mountain that
morning to the day O. S. Pettingill had handed him a tape
recorder, or, later, his encounter with the Bewick's wren
singing in his backyard in Oregon. As they talked, Hamilton
asked Kroodsma if he had heard the other bellbird nearby. Its
call sounded more like a *quack* than a *bonk,* she said. As she
described it, Kroodsma realized he had indeed heard it, but
it sounded so different from the *bonk* that he hadn't thought
it was a bellbird. Although the bellbird's range extends
from western Panama through Costa Rica and into eastern
Nicaragua, there were, Hamilton explained, three apparently
distinct populations. Kroodsma would eventually learn that the
Monteverde population, named for the mountain village near
their breeding grounds, produces the call most people are
familiar with—the loud *bonk*. The Talamanca population, from
the region of the same name near the Panama border, gives a
call that sounds like a *quack*. A third population existed in
Nicaragua, but less was known about its vocalizations. Hamilton had often heard birds in the Monteverde area using the
Talamanca dialect, the *quack*. Such different vocalizations,
Kroodsma felt, could only be explained in two ways. Either

the birds were different species, despite their identical appearance, or they were learning their vocalizations. The former wouldn't be unheard of. The willow and alder flycatchers that Kroodsma had studied were once considered one species, Traill's flycatcher, until relatively recently when the American Ornithologists' Union decided otherwise, based in large part on the different songs of the two. The latter possibility was more interesting of course. "I was just dumbstruck," Kroodsma says. "At that moment I knew there were questions to be answered. My instinct was that they were learning, but of course there was nothing to back that up."

Kroodsma forgot about his wish list and drove to Las Alturas, a Stanford University field station at the Panama border, where he, Sanchez, Stemple, and Byers recorded bellbirds with the Talamanca dialect. Then they drove back into Costa Rica's central highlands to Monteverde, where they searched for birds with the Monteverde dialect. The bellbirds near Monteverde were sparse, but Debra Hamilton, who lived in Monteverde, told Kroodsma that in July and August the bellbirds congregated in and around the village and would be easy to record, so Kroodsma made plans to return to Costa Rica the following year.

A couple of months later at home in Amherst, Kroodsma received a message from a Brazilian acquaintance, Hernan Fandino, who asked if Kroodsma might send him some bird bands. In the exchange that followed, Kroodsma asked Hernan what he knew about bellbirds. There were four species of bellbirds—the three-wattled, white, bearded, and bare-throated. Though their appearances differed, they shared many traits. The bare-throated bellbird, Kroodsma knew, was found in Brazil. Hernan told Kroodsma that the bare-throated bellbird was beloved for its call, and there was, in fact, a town named for it, Arapongas. Many people in Arapongas kept caged bare-throated bellbirds. Kroodsma told Hernan he would not only send him some bird bands but also money to take his wife out to dinner in Arapongas if he would visit the town and learn what he could of the bare-throated bellbird's vocalizations. A few weeks later, Hernan strolled through Arapongas, asking about bellbirds. One in particular caught his attention. This bellbird had been given to its present owner because the man who'd raised it from a baby was displeased that the bellbird didn't sing a proper bellbird song. Instead, it sang a partial bellbird song into which it mixed the songs of the blackbirds it had been raised with. This, of course, was not possible if, like other suboscines, the bellbird was born with its song.

The following year in mid-July, Kroodsma loaded up his equipment and headed for Costa Rica, accompanied once again by his good friend Dave Stemple. I met them in Monteverde a couple of days later. Kroodsma's plan was to familiarize himself with the bellbird's vocalizations and record as many different bellbirds as he could. At the same time, Debra Hamilton was capturing bellbirds in mist nets and banding them, part of a study begun in 1992 when George Powell, now a senior scientist with the World Wildlife Fund and a longtime resident of Monteverde, became concerned about the apparent decline in the bellbird population. Powell initiated the research, then turned it over to Hamilton a couple of years later. The results of the study and Hamilton's knowledge of the birds would be critical to Kroodsma's research. Most important, if Kroodsma could locate and record some of the bellbirds Hamilton had banded, he would be able to analyze vocalizations of known birds and correlate this to various factors. Knowing a bird's age, for instance, might provide some insight into how the bellbird's song develops. One interesting thing about the bellbird is its slow maturation. A first-year male three-wattled bellbird is olive green and essentially wattleless. Small wattles begin to develop in the second year, growing longer year by year until they are full length in year four. At this point the bird's coloration, which has been changing subtly, begins to change more dramatically, a mottled brown appearing in its green chest. By year five, its head is a muddy white and the green has given way to a dull brown. At year six its stunning two-tone plumage is nearly complete. A seven-year maturation is unheard of for passerines. Furthermore, it seems to take several years for the birds to perfect their song, Hamilton said. The process is similar, though much slower, to song development by young songbirds.

Kroodsma considered what he knew: there were three different "dialects"; a related species in Brazil learned blackbird vocalizations; and the bellbird's song took several years to develop. All of this suggested that the three-wattled bellbird learned its song. Kroodsma was ever mindful though of his own warning: "We 'know' too much." So far he had only the kind of information scientists refer to as anecdotal evidence: stories and random observations. It was no more scientific than a rumor. On the other hand, if Kroodsma recorded enough bellbirds over several years he might be able to assemble the empirical evidence science demanded. Demonstrating that a suboscine learned its vocalizations would be news of the first order in avian bioacoustics, and a hallmark in Kroodsma's career.

Raising baby bellbirds in the laboratory, of course, would likely provide irrefutable evidence of song learning, if it was taking place. But Kroodsma entertained the notion only briefly. There were two problems with it, one practical, the other ethical. Although Hamilton and others had been studying the bellbird for nearly a decade, only five nests had ever been located. What's more, the bellbird population was declining, most likely in response to deforestation. From years of censuses, Hamilton estimated the Monteverde population of the three-wattled bellbird at only seven hundred birds. Kroodsma could not have convinced himself to remove birds from such an endangered population even if it were possible.

On my first morning with Kroodsma in the summer of 1999, I met him on a farm road outside Monteverde. The village is situated just below the continental divide in the mountains that run like a spine up the center of Costa Rica. A popular ecotourism destination, it is renowned for a cloud-forest preserve on its outskirts and as a place one can see the resplendent quetzal, a glittering green bird with a red breast and a spectacular thirty-inch train of tail feathers, considered by many the most beautiful bird in the Western Hemisphere. As a result, the amenities in Monteverde included comfortable lodging and good food. It seemed too easy to rise from a restful night's sleep in a pleasant lodge and drive a couple of miles to a site where bellbirds were plentiful. When I arrived at the appointed hour, 5:30 A.M., Kroodsma was waiting. Daylight was beginning to spill into the valley through a light mist. We stood beside the cars for a few minutes, talking about what we saw—hundreds of acres of land cleared for cattle and crops on both sides of the dirt road, except for a ten-acre island of rain forest bordering the road on its south edge. This forest remnant and much of the land around it was part of Finca Las Americas, a farm owned by a family sympathetic to Hamilton's bellbird research. Kroodsma had permission to work on the property, so we slipped through a barbwire fence and entered the forest, following a trail that led through the heart of it. Somewhere ahead of us, bellbirds were calling. It took only a few minutes to walk through the patch of forest and come out into a cleared plot of land on the other side. There, a line of trees arced around three sides of the clearing, which was dotted with freshly dug holes where coffee trees would be planted.

Through the open edge of the clearing I could see grassy pastures carved on mountain slopes in the distance and a few low-lying clouds drifting in the valleys between ridges. Only small stands of trees remained of what was once a continuous expanse of montane rain forest. The Pacific slope of Costa Rica's central mountain range is less rugged than the Atlantic slope, and its weather is milder. As a result, the mountainsides and valleys on this side of the Tilaran Mountains had been cleared more extensively than those on the Atlantic slope. One of the things George Powell had discovered when he began studying the bellbird was that it made a complex altitudinal migration. Powell placed radio transmitters on birds and eventually mapped their migration route, which, it turned out, circled much of central Costa Rica. In June, after breeding on the Atlantic slope just beyond Monteverde, the birds cross over the continental divide and descend a few hundred feet to forests on the Pacific slope in and around Monteverde. There they congregate for a couple of months, then fly back across the continental divide, descending to sea level on the Atlantic coast near the Nicaraguan border. A few months later they make a cross-country flight back over the mountains to the Pacific lowlands. And then, two months later, they return to Monteverde to breed and begin the cycle once more. The problem is that forests on the Pacific slope continue to be cut down. In many areas all that remain are small parcels like the one Kroodsma and I had just walked through. This particular forest remnant appears to be particularly important to the bellbirds. Hamilton believes that in some years more than half the males in the Monteverde population make use of it at some point during July and August.

As soon as we entered the clearing, Kroodsma's attention turned to a bellbird calling from high in a tree on the south edge. Kroodsma stopped, raised his parabola toward the bird, and turned on the tape recorder. I raised my binoculars to get a look at the bird I had so far only heard about. This bird, a mature adult, was perched on a bare branch. He leaned forward slightly like a downhill skier, then opened his bill so wide the lower mandible nearly touched his chest, exposing a mouth as black as a cave—a striking contrast to the bird's snow-white head. No sound emerged though. For two or three seconds—it seemed much longer—the bellbird remained frozen in this posture, its mouth open, almost unhinged it seemed, appearing for all the world like a bird about to cough up a mango. The muscles on the bird's neck and upper back swelled and contracted. His chest heaved. His throat rippled. Still, his mouth was agape. Then, as if someone had sneaked up behind the bellbird and squeezed him, he emitted an explosive *bonk*. The call reverberated through the trees, a sound unlike any I'd ever heard. If frogs were bellmakers, their bells would sound like this.

The loud *bonk* was followed by three whistles that reminded me of a starling's squeaks, something so different from the *bonk* it was difficult to believe they were coming from the same bird. The bellbird's mouth remained wide open all the while, which created the impression that the whistles were the last bit of sound this bird could eke out before it needed to catch its breath. Finally, the bellbird closed its mouth. Later, listening through Kroodsma's parabolic microphone, I would hear the soft, swishing sounds that came between the whistles. Other birds may be better singers, but none could give a more spellbinding performance. Something about the tone and explosiveness of the loud *bonk* was mesmerizing. It reverberated in the trees, a singular exclamation of . . . what? Breeding season was over, so it wasn't likely this bird was calling to defend a territory or attract a female. Yet it must be something important because the bellbird calls like this over and over from early morning to dusk, two thousand songs per day, for at least nine months of the year. One bird calling would have been enough to keep me transfixed for some time, but I could hear half a dozen other bellbirds calling from various points around the clearing. One *bonk* rang out through the cloud-darkened skies, then another in the distance, then two more that overlapped each other—a mountainside of bell towers. Why the bellbird is so vociferous no one knows. At moments in the days to come though, I couldn't help but imagine the bellbirds were tolling a requiem for their disappearing forests.

On that first morning, Kroodsma had no trouble locating bellbirds. He had just the opposite problem—so many bellbirds he didn't know where to turn. He recorded one bellbird, then another, moving a few steps that way, then back a few paces this way, turning north, then west, following the bellbirds. I followed Kroodsma, trying to ignore the swallow-tailed kite circling overhead and the big keel-billed toucan that kept bringing his fruit basket of colors to a dead tree in the clearing. Kroodsma moved slowly, freezing in motion when he recorded. Once Kroodsma turned on the tape recorder, he was expressionless. He looked straight ahead at the bellbird, but it was a blank stare. His mind was elsewhere, focused on the sounds coming through his earphones and on adjusting the recorder's controls. He was wearing high, black rubber boots, blue work pants, a camouflage shirt, and a baseball cap. From a strap slung over his right shoulder, a bag dangled at his hip, giving him easy access to extra cassette tapes, various recording equipment, and the small dictation tape recorder he used for note taking. On his left side was his tape recorder, housed in a dark blue bag held by a padded shoulder strap. To all of this, Kroodsma added a small JanSport daypack on his back, which carried extra batteries, a rain poncho, and other miscellaneous items. As always, earphones rested on his head over the baseball cap, and binoculars dangled against his chest. A cable ran from the earphones to the tape recorder, an HHB Portadat machine Greg Budney had lent him. A second cable ran from the Portadat to a Telinga parabolic microphone system. He held the parabola away from his body, but kept his arm at a ninety-degree angle at the elbow so the upper arm was as much at rest as possible. He told me once that he did exercises in the winter to strengthen the hand he used to hold the parabola so he could keep it steady for long periods.

All morning he recorded from the clearing as bellbirds flew in and out of the surrounding trees. He knew he was likely recording the same few individuals coming back to perches they favored. It would be best to move to another location, but he could not make himself leave. There were just too many bellbirds here, and he didn't know what he'd find if he went somewhere else. Once, as he turned off his recorder and looked about, trying to decide which bellbird to record next, he looked at me and spoke in a voice of delighted weariness: "I've been sucked into the black hole of bellbirds."

Not all the days in July 1999 were so productive. Weather was a problem. In Costa Rica the rainy season extends from May through November, and July is one of the wettest months, not a good time to be carrying a tape recorder in the forest. The highest slopes around Monteverde, just under six thousand feet, are cloud-covered much of the time. On the other hand, during the dry season—a relative term: Monteverde receives on average ninety-six inches of rainfall annually—the bellbirds are far less accessible. The first year of recording was a learning experience. Weather aside, Kroodsma came away feeling confident he could gather enough recordings in the next two or three years to prove the bellbirds were learning their songs.

In addition to Finca Las Americas, Kroodsma recorded bellbirds at two other farms and a tourist attraction known as Finca Ecologica. He got recordings of many birds singing the Monteverde dialect and some singing the Talamanca dialect, and he recorded bellbirds at each stage of development from birds in their second year to adults in full plumage. The second-year birds produced primarily parrotlike squawks, which were sometimes mixed with sounds that seemed to belong to the Monteverde dialect or the Talamanca dialect. Most interesting though, Kroodsma came across birds that combined both dialects. He referred to them as "bilingual" singers. He wondered if the bilingual singers, all juveniles, were trying out both dialects, then choosing one of them when they reached adulthood. And if so, how did they make that choice? What influenced them? There was nothing like this in any of the literature on birdsong, and it was the most convincing evidence so far that the bellbird learned its vocalizations.

Best of all, Kroodsma discovered he was able to locate and record some of the banded birds. It was often difficult to determine the band combination of a bird perched high in a tree–even with Dave Stemple's sixty-power scope trained on him–but Kroodsma ended up with recordings of six birds whose bands he and Stemple saw clearly. Sonograms of known individuals would be supremely valuable. From listening to birds as he recorded them, and later from looking closely at sonograms, he could tell that the Monteverde singers sang three different songs and the Talamanca two. What's more, all of the Monteverde singers agreed on the song's details with considerable consistency. The same was true of the Talamanca singers. When he compared the Talamanca songs recorded at Monteverde with those recorded at Las Alturas, they were the same. This demonstrated beyond any reasonable doubt that two distinct dialects were sung by two different groups of birds of the same species. And by now Kroodsma believed there was only one species.

Near the end of the 1999 trip, I accompanied Kroodsma to a meeting Debra Hamilton arranged to discuss the July bellbird census. Fourteen local natural history guides took a day off from leading tours to count bellbirds. Each walked a pre-determined transect, listening for bellbirds. Now they sat in chairs along the walls of a small room at Finca Ecologica and announced the results as Hamilton recorded them on a chart. In the end, the figures were disappointing. A total of 87 birds had been found on the Pacific slope. Last year the count was 128. The year before, it was 153. This might be a natural fluctuation in the population or somehow related to the difficulties of people hiking through the forest and trying to count bellbirds high in the trees. But George Powell, who slipped quietly into the room halfway through the meeting, shook his head when he heard the figures. "The population is just a fragment of what it once was," he said softly. Powell, a thin, wiry man whose extensive experience in the neotropics and tireless advocacy of sensible conservation has earned him great respect, thought the bellbirds were in serious trouble. Despite Costa Rica's much praised system of national parks and biological reserves—which protects roughly 12 percent of its land (the United States, by comparison, protects about 3.5 percent of its land)—roughly half of Costa Rica's forests have been cut down since 1940. Moreover, the great majority of what is protected lies high in the mountains. Lower montane forests, particularly those favored by bellbirds, fall into the "coffee belt," the land best suited for crops. Little of this forest type remains. Next to nothing is protected.

The remaining forest, and nearly all of it that is protected, falls on the Atlantic slopes whose steep ravines and narrow valleys make them less favorable for development. Because the bellbird's migration takes it on a wide loop through central Costa Rica, both highlands and lowlands, land preservation needs to be distributed more evenly among habitat types. "In theory, Costa Rica is committed to maintaining 90 percent of its biodiversity," Powell said. "In theory." The steady decline of the bellbird population gave Kroodsma's work some urgency, and it presented the possibility for a terrible irony—Kroodsma would succeed in proving that the bellbird was learning its song only to see the bird disappear from the forest forever.

Having gathered promising evidence a suboscine was learning like an oscine, Kroodsma applied to the National Science Foundation for a grant to fund the bellbird research he envisioned for the next few years. He had received one NSF grant after another throughout his career, so he was optimistic, particularly given the importance of his findings. A few months later, he was taken aback when his proposal was rejected. The review board was skeptical. Most of Kroodsma's evidence was anecdotal or unsubstantiated, they said. Moreover, Kroodsma should be raising bellbirds in the laboratory if he wanted to prove they learned to sing.

Kroodsma was surprised, but he was too fascinated by the bellbird to let this stop him. The following July he returned to Monteverde and recorded bellbirds for a week. Once again, he located several banded bellbirds, and once again he found juvenile bellbirds that were bilingual. At home in Amherst after this second trip to Monteverde, he contacted colleagues around the world and asked them for information on bellbirds. In particular, did they know of any recordings? Still, he wanted at least one more year's worth of data, so he planned another trip to Monteverde for July 2001. Now that he had more data, he revised his grant proposal and sent it back to NSF. Again he was rejected. Although one reviewer wrote,

"Over the last twenty-five years, [Kroodsma] has contributed more to the study of the function and development of avian vocalizations than any other person," the negative comments outweighed the positive. One, in particular, troubled Kroodsma: "[The] lack of laboratory tutoring was certainly a weakness . . . despite [Kroodsma's] concern about conservation ethics," and the data "were poorly documented and subject to obvious other interpretations."

"I'd like to know of just one other reasonable explanation," Kroodsma said. "If I had proposed to put bellbirds in cages and study them, or shoot fifty bellbirds and dissect their brains, I'd probably have gotten the grant. The grant reviewers are coming from a tradition of sound chambers in the lab. They can't get beyond canaries and zebra finches." Kroodsma told me this as we drove out of the lowlands of Costa Rica and into the mountains. It was July 2001. We had met at the airport in Miami and flown to San José, met Julio Sanchez, rented a car, and were off for a week of recording in Monteverde to be followed by a journey to Nicaragua to try to find the bellbirds from the third population that so little was known about. Kroodsma's thoughts had flowed toward his lack of funding as we discussed the cost of renting the car. Thinking of the grant reviewers' comments angered him. He had also run into skeptics at a talk he gave at Rockefeller University a few weeks earlier. He began by saying the bellbird was clearly learning its song. That was a mistake, Kroodsma said. Saying it with that kind of certainty made them try to disprove it. "They kept latching onto one point or another and not seeing the whole picture," he said. "They asked also if I was going to capture bellbirds and study them in the laboratory under controlled conditions, and I said, 'Absolutely not.'"

Kroodsma paused a moment, then shrugged this off. His face brightened, self-consciously at first, then with genuine pleasure as he imagined the bellbirds that awaited us. He was eager to find out how many banded birds Debra Hamilton had found on the most recent census, and he wanted to begin recording first thing the next morning. Earlier, when we'd arrived in San José, my luggage was missing, but Kroodsma couldn't wait to get out of the airport and on the road. He saw no reason to hang around the airport for a couple of hours when we could be making our way toward the kingdom of the bellbirds.

We drove northwest into the mountains along a winding, narrow highway crumbling at the edges and pitted with potholes, neither of which discouraged the locals from passing two or three cars at a time as they sped around blind curves. In midafternoon, we turned off the highway and headed north into the heart of the Tilaran Mountains. The final twenty miles to Monteverde took two hours. We lurched along at a snail's pace over a roadbed composed of great, jagged chunks of rock, many of them the size of bricks, some as big as cinder blocks, laid down, I guessed, to prevent erosion. This section of the central mountain range, the Tilaran Mountains, didn't rise as high as the mountains did elsewhere, where several peaks reach more than ten thousand feet. Here the continental divide was less than six thousand feet. The broad valleys of the Pacific slope had a bucolic beauty, deadly as it was: wide-open, grassy pastures were fringed with the darker, rumpled green of what was left of the primary forest. Dairy farming was a major enterprise around Monteverde, settled by North American Quaker families in the 1950s who were attracted to Costa Rica's climate and its pacifist tradition (the country abolished its army in 1948).

Arriving in Monteverde in late afternoon, we turned onto the farm road to Finca Las Americas. Within a stone's throw of the farm was a newly constructed conservation center with facilities to house visiting scientists and conservation groups.

Kroodsma was delighted to stay so close to where the bellbirds gathered. The conservation center was four simple, attractive buildings built atop a ridge with a stunning view of the Pacific slope—ridge after ridge with puffy clouds hovering over them, and in the distance, just visible, a faint glimmer that was the Pacific Ocean. It was a reminder of how small Costa Rica is, no bigger than West Virginia; all of Central America is only a slip of land that rose slowly from the oceans 4 million years ago. Kroodsma and I settled into a room with a large window facing this vista, and Julio took another room. Not long after we had unpacked, Debra Hamilton arrived to have dinner with us, as did Danilo Brenes, a natural history guide Kroodsma had hired to help us spot bellbirds. Danilo, a handsome young man with dark, expressive eyes, had helped Hamilton band bellbirds in years past. He was everything one could hope for in a guide: knowledgeable, sharp-eyed, friendly, and energetic. When I met him in 1999, he seemed shy, but in fact he was only reluctant to talk much because, he said, his English was not good. Now he was talkative and at ease, and his English much improved. He had worked on it with the help of a North American girlfriend who lived in Monteverde.

We talked throughout dinner of mutual friends and shared interests until Kroodsma could not contain his bellbird fever any longer. His meal unfinished, he pushed his plate aside and made room for a notebook he retrieved from the daypack at his feet. Debra Hamilton had completed a census only five days earlier, timed to benefit Kroodsma's recording. She was expecting Kroodsma's questions. "I can't wait any longer," Kroodsma said. "I have to know about the birds. Are they back at Mariano's?"

"Ohhh, yesss," Debra said, smiling. "And they are at Stuckey's too." Mariano Arguedas owned Finca Las Americas, which included the site Kroodsma had dubbed "the black hole of bellbirds" in 1999. The forest fragment on the farm where the bellbirds congregated was only a couple of hundred yards away, so if the birds were plentiful there this year, then it should be relatively easy to record them. The bellbirds seemed to cluster in certain areas in alternate years, possibly because their favorite food, a small, wild avocado from trees in the Lauraceae family, fruited biannually.

Debra got out a piece of paper with a chart of the census results.

"How about Azul/Oro–Oro/Azul?" Kroodsma asked. "Was he back at Finca Ecologica?"

"No. We didn't see him."

This was a bird that Kroodsma had recorded at length in 1999. If he could find him again and get more high-quality recordings, he'd have some especially valuable data. Debra slowly went down the list of banded birds while Kroodsma noted their locations and checked his own list to see if any of them were birds he had recorded in the past. They continued to talk about particular birds, using their band combinations like the names of old friends. In a sense, they were. In the days to come I would begin to appreciate this more than I had. Each bird was a unique individual, not just a bellbird. This was so obvious it was startling to realize how often I tended to think of Kroodsma's research as something in the abstract—a study that would show that suboscines too may learn vocalizations. Kroodsma thinks this way much of the time as well, but he doesn't forget that all abstract scientific thinking arises from the physical world, in his case, particular birds. Some of the bellbirds have long histories, making them all the more interesting. One banded bird is known to be at least sixteen years old, and Debra Hamilton believes they likely live twenty to thirty years, perhaps more.

As the dinner plates were cleared from the table, Kroodsma looked over the notes he had just made. "Where should we go first? What would make the most sense?"

Debra spoke up. "Oh, I forgot to tell you. There's some sad news. Jorge has lost ownership of Finca Ecologica. He has to sign papers tomorrow, giving the property to the new owner." Finca Ecologica, or the "ecology farm," was a nature tour operation run by a local family. Hamilton explained that a woman from the United States claimed, successfully, that she held rights to the property, so now it wasn't clear what would happen to the place and whether Kroodsma would be allowed to continue recording there. "You should go tomorrow morning and record," Debra said. "They are signing the papers at noon."

This made Kroodsma's decision about what to do on the first day simple if unpleasant. He would get to the farm, hope for good weather, and record as many bellbirds as possible.

Our schedule for the next two weeks would be determined by the bellbirds' schedule, and the weather. By now I was accustomed, if never quite acclimated, to Kroodsma's penchant to get up and be out in the field before the birds themselves were awake. On these days I thought of myself as living in a special part of the world that existed in Kroodsma Savings Time. I was not unhappy that the three-wattled bellbird is not a typical predawn singer. Because the bellbird sings continually from dawn to dusk, Kroodsma had all day to record. It meant the days would be long, but it also meant we would be able to sleep later than usual. "Let's get up at four-thirty," Kroodsma said. "That should be early enough. We can be on our way by five."

Kroodsma's goal was simply to gather more representative samples of bellbird vocalizations from as many different birds as possible, but especially from banded individuals. As wild as the bellbirds are, this fieldwork was generally tame. From nature programs on television–filled with manufactured drama and the hushed hyperbole of a narrator–we tend to think of zoological fieldwork as high adventure filled with danger and discovery. Most fieldwork, in fact, is like Kroodsma's: slow and repetitive. Kroodsma needed not derring-do but unwavering concentration and persistence to do his work. On some days we stood for long periods in a clearing, recording bellbirds in the trees along the margins. Half an hour could seem like an hour, and as Kroodsma recorded a bellbird, then turned to record another, moving a few paces this way and that way, turning slowly as he aimed the parabolic microphone, I sometimes felt like one of the last pieces on a life-size chessboard. Sometimes, the silence of the work seemed the most conspicuous thing about it. I grew so accustomed to not speaking while Kroodsma was recording that I often couldn't find my voice in the intervals between and was content to move through the morning wordlessly.

On the first morning, we arrived at Finca Ecologica shortly after dawn. Kroodsma and Julio briefly discussed which areas to cover and when to meet back at the car, then walked off in different directions. Kroodsma was carrying the HHB Porta-dat recorder he had used in previous years. When he published his data, this would eliminate any criticism from skeptical reviewers that different equipment somehow affected the recordings. In addition to the camouflage clothes he routinely wore when recording the bellbirds, he had placed more camouflage material over the parabolic dish, attaching it to the rim with small binder clips. Kroodsma had come to believe the bellbirds were disturbed by light reflecting off the dish. He enjoyed using simple materials to solve problems with the expensive, sophisticated equipment. Two more binder clips held a piece of tubular aluminum he had bent like a pipe cleaner to make a gun sight for aiming the parabolic dish. Finally, a section of a coat hanger was attached near the handle of the parabola so Kroodsma could hang the dish at his waist if he needed to free up both hands.

We headed south along a path toward a bellbird calling from somewhere high in the trees, Danilo leading the way. In dark work pants and a plain T-shirt, carrying a tripod-mounted spotting scope over his shoulder, Danilo moved with a light step. Besides the scope, the only other thing he carried with him were the color plates from *The Birds of Costa Rica,* which he had stripped from the book and sewn together to make a handy pictorial guide, though he rarely needed it. Danilo had grown up in Monteverde. The forests were his backyard. His sharp, inquisitive mind belied the fact that, like many of the youth in the area, he had not finished high school. The value of an education seemed limited since a future in Monteverde held few opportunities besides working on one of the area's dairy farms. When he was seventeen, Danilo was hired as a research assistant for a few months by George Powell, who recognized his native intelligence. By the time Danilo was in his midtwenties, ecotourism had swept into Monteverde and he was making a living as a natural history guide. Now thirty years old, he was one of the most knowledgeable guides in the area. Danilo's job with Kroodsma was to locate a position from which he could see the bellbird through the scope, determine its age by looking closely at its color pattern, and look for bands on the bird's legs.

The first bird of the morning had no bands, so Kroodsma spent little time recording him, moving on to a second bird, also unbanded. A short while later, a third bird appeared, this one an adult in full plumage sitting in clear view. An adult bellbird was always a compelling sight. The immaculate white of his head was regal, and the black wattles were weirdly beautiful jewelry. They dangled loosely, one from each side of the base of the bill and the third from the top of the bill. When the bird changed positions on the branch, it often fluttered its wings as it hopped into the air and pivoted 180 degrees in a movement that was part flight, part gymnastics. As it did so, its wattles flew about, swinging wildly. Sometimes it jerked its head as if to fling the wattles for all to see. This could have interesting results. Debra Hamilton has seen one bird with its center wattle in a knot.

By eight-thirty Kroodsma figured he and Julio had recorded all of the bellbirds in the area, none of which were banded, so we drove to a preserve near Bosque Eterno, a tract of land preserved by the Quaker settlers and now managed by The Monteverde Conservation League. Debra Hamilton's census last week had found a banded bird in this area. Julio and Kroodsma split up again, agreeing to meet back at the car by noon. Kroodsma and Danilo set off down a trail known as Calandria, a common name for the bellbird. The banded bellbird had been seen near trail marker number 14. The trees here were mature, towering over us, the undergrowth rich, varied, and deeply shadowed. We walked silently, the trail following a ridge, descending gradually for the most part with only short sections that were steep and required careful footwork. We were not far from Monteverde, but none of the village sounds reached us, no distant motors. The cathedral silence of the forest was broken only by occasional scuffling noises in the underbrush—agoutis perhaps, the plump, tail-less rodents common in much of the New World tropics. And I heard the songs of rufous-and-white wrens, a common bird with a beautiful melody, sweet and a bit melancholy. It is a series of low, whistled notes, ghostly, almost owl-like, slow, then faster, then a single note rising slightly. In the days to come, we'd hear the wren often. Its song seemed to follow us. Its soft tones coming from the understory were a counterpoint to the bellbird's ringing exclamation from the treetops. Kroodsma rarely stopped to listen to anything but a bellbird. Toucans flew overhead and he ignored them. Blue-crowned motmots sat in clear view along the trails calling their name, and he only glanced their way. Large tropical hummingbirds whizzed past our heads like jeweled shooting stars. Parrots barreled across the sky, drawing an arc like a green rainbow that ended in a pot of more green high in the trees. And always there were brown jays, raucous, big as crows and hard to ignore, moving from tree to tree like street gangs. Kroodsma saw and heard only bellbirds.

At trail marker 13 Kroodsma slowed up, and as if on cue, a bellbird called. Kroodsma raised the parabola, holding it out ahead of him. Danilo slipped into the undergrowth off the trail. In a few moments we were almost directly under the bird, but Kroodsma could not see him. The ridge we were on was narrow and we were near its western edge. Kroodsma worked his way through a few feet of undergrowth and came to the edge of the ridge, where we looked out on the tops of trees growing on the slope below. The slope was too steep to move down it easily, and if we stepped into the open, we might startle the bird, so Kroodsma craned his neck, trying to find a sight line. The bellbird was thirty feet or so above us in the crown of one of the trees growing on the edge of the ridge. Kroodsma turned on his recorder. The bird called loudly, but was facing away from us. He was likely on a perch that looked out across the valley, and had we been on the ridge on the other side of the valley, we'd have a clear, if distant, view of him. Danilo, circling the area, could catch only glimpses of him. When Kroodsma paused in his recording, Danilo told him that he got a look at the bird's feet. He was banded. This was almost certainly the banded bird that the census had turned up. But Kroodsma was not willing to make that assumption, and in fact he did not look at his chart to see what the band combination should be.

Most of the bellbirds that Debra had banded over the years had two bands on each leg. The bands might be any one of several colors, and they were "read" from top to bottom and from left leg to right. Typically the colors were given in Spanish and abbreviated in writing. Danilo told Kroodsma he thought this bird was Azul/Plata–Rojo/Oro, or A/P–R/O: blue above silver on the left leg and red above gold on the right leg. Danilo wasn't certain though. It was difficult to see the bird at all, let alone see both legs. Although sometimes bellbirds perched in the open, just as often they sat on a branch inside the crown of a tree, in which case the sight line Danilo found through the leaves might provide only a small window on the bird. And since the bellbirds moved about as they called, they moved in and out of view, one moment framed by leaves, the next visible only partially or not at all. Band colors were sometimes difficult to make out, and occasionally their intensity would change before one's eyes as the lighting changed. Sunlight reflecting off bands brightened some colors and obscured others. Silver bands often looked green when they reflected foliage. Dull, indirect light was generally good for light colors, but darker colors were then less distinct.

Kroodsma noted Danilo's initial determination of the bands, then continued recording. The bellbird called regularly, but also moved about, making it difficult for Kroodsma to get a clear recording. Then, suddenly, a juvenile bellbird joined the adult, landing on the same perch. The young bird sat silently. Danilo move his tripod a few inches, repositioned the scope, and looked again at the birds. Now, he said, the bands on the right leg looked to be Azul/Plata, not Rojo/Oro, but still he wasn't certain. It was important, of course, that Kroodsma knew the band combination without any doubts, so Danilo continued to peer through his scope at the bellbird's legs. Now and then he looked down and fingered what appeared to be a bracelet on his left wrist. There, on a string, were one each of all the different colored bands that had been used on the bellbirds over the years. Being able to look at the bands diminished the chance for mistakes.

After half an hour, the bird moved to a new perch in a tree nearly directly above us. Danilo repositioned the scope and got a better view of the bird's legs. Once more the colors looked different than they had moments ago, but this time Danilo thought he was seeing them correctly. Rather than say what he'd seen, he asked me to look as well, hoping I would come to the same conclusion independently. Positioning the scope so the bird was in view often left it in an awkward position for the viewer. Trying to align my eye with the eyepiece gave me new-found respect for the contortions Danilo put himself through each day. The eyepiece was perhaps five feet off the ground, too high for me to get on my knees and look up, and too low for me to simply bend over. I squatted like a weight lifter in midlift, tilted my head back until my neck would take no more, then tried to hold steady and focus all my attention on what I saw. For a couple of seconds I had trouble seeing the bellbird at all, but then I saw part of his chest and his head through the leaves that surrounded him like a wreath. How Danilo had found this opening to look through I could not imagine. The bellbird shifted a bit and more of him came into view. One of his legs was visible. The top band looked blue, the bottom band, silver—Azul/Plata, which was what Danilo had seen on the left leg. But the bird's legs were in shadows. He moved on his perch, and now I could see only his upper body. Again he moved. Both legs came into view and I strained to see the colors on the right leg, comparing them to the colors of the left. Still the light was dim, and it was difficult to distinguish any color at all now. Several minutes passed—my legs beginning to wobble from the strain—and then, suddenly, the bird turned around completely just as the sun came out from behind a cloud and lit his perch. The bands now were clearer: Azul/Plata–Azul/Oro. I was as sure as I could be. Yes, Danilo said. That was what he'd seen.

Now that he had a banded bird, Kroodsma took his time. He continued recording, aware it was already half an hour past when he had agreed to meet Julio at the car. In the morning,

Terri Mallory, our host at the bellbird conservation center, had given Kroodsma and Julio walkie-talkies, but Kroodsma had already discovered that the mountain ridges blocked the signals. He tried again to reach Julio, but got no answer. The original plan was to return to the station for lunch, then go back out and record some more, but now Kroodsma debated with himself: "If we take a break now, we will lose ninety minutes of recording time. And if we don't go back out until two or so, and the bellbirds stop calling at four, we won't get much. Leaving now, though, is the only sensible thing to do. But it hurts. Julio is waiting for us back at the car."

While Kroodsma was thinking aloud, Danilo had walked farther down the trail, so Kroodsma set off to retrieve him, but fifteen minutes later Danilo returned without Kroodsma. They had located another bellbird, and this one was banded too. Returning to the car was out of the question. A hundred yards down the trail, Kroodsma stood with the microphone trained on the bellbird, a bird with only one band on each leg: Verde/Verde. Kroodsma recorded for nearly half an hour, then stopped to debate again if he should continue recording or go back to meet Julio. Breakfast had been at 4 A.M. Lunch was long overdue. "But we can eat lunch anytime, right?" Kroodsma said. "Should we just record while we can?" Finally, he shrugged and without a word started back up the trail.

At one-thirty, nearing the head of the trail, we came across Julio. After waiting at the car for an hour, he had decided to come looking for us. Now he teased Kroodsma, saying he tried repeatedly to get him on the walkie-talkie, but finally gave up and just left the walkie-talkie back at the car. Julio was smiling, but he was also clearly unhappy. Kroodsma apologized, explaining the trouble we had had seeing the colors of the bands on the first banded bird, and then there was the second banded bird. A few minutes later, Julio and Danilo stopped on the trail for a moment while Kroodsma and I walked back to the car. There, Kroodsma fretted more: "The first day, and I'm already in trouble with Julio. He puts up with me. You can't stop recording when you have two banded birds. It doesn't work that way. I'm afraid we'll get three days of rain and that will be that."

Back at the station, Kroodsma heard bellbirds calling in the distance at Finca Las Americas. While Julio and I took our time eating lunch, then took showers, Kroodsma strapped on his recording gear and set off walking down the entrance road toward the bellbirds. Two hours later he returned, walking slowly up the path to the porch, where he stopped at the first step. He gently set down the parabola, bent over, and slipped the daypack off his back and the bag off his right shoulder, then lifted the strap off his left shoulder and lowered the tape recorder carefully to the ground at his feet. Having shed the weight he'd been carrying, he suddenly seemed unable to move. He stood motionless, hunched over, a blank expression on his face. It was five o'clock, twelve hours after we'd set out this morning. "Here I am," he said, "standing here trying to figure out what is the most efficient way to carry all of this equipment into the room, and I'm too tired to make a decision."

And still the day was not over. In the morning Kroodsma had noticed some electronic noise coming from the recording system. It wasn't enough to affect the recording he'd done today, but if it got worse, it might show up on the sonograms later or, worse yet, the system might fail entirely. After a shower Kroodsma carried the parabola out to the porch, sat down at a table, and began to dismantle it. The noise, he thought, was coming from the microphone. There was a problem though. The microphone and parabolic dish were an integrated system. Ordinarily, one didn't replace parts, but replaced the entire system. Kroodsma thought, however, that he might be able to rig a different mike in the parabola, and he had brought along with him just what he needed: a rubber drain hose from a washing machine. Now he slipped the faulty microphone out of the small sleeve that held it in position. The microphone that he wanted to use as a replacement had a smaller diameter, so Kroodsma cut off a section of the rubber hose, split it down the middle with his knife, and inserted it into the sleeve. Then he placed the new microphone inside the rubber hose. Still the microphone wiggled a bit. From his repair kit, an assortment of materials he always carried with him, Kroodsma pulled out a strip of thin foam, cut a piece from it, and wrapped it tightly around the mike, then placed it back in the tubing. Now the new microphone fit snugly. It would remain in place just fine. Kroodsma then replaced the original microphone. He would keep the rubber hose and second mike in his shoulder bag, knowing that he could change them in the field in a few minutes if necessary.

In the dining area on a dry-erase board Terri Mallory used for phone messages was what looked like a crude road map. A single road began at the bottom of the board, rose upward a short distance, then split into two long roads, forming a long, loosely drawn *Y*. This was the simplified map of the evolutionary lineage of oscines and suboscines Kroodsma had quickly sketched last night when Terri Mallory asked why he was so interested in whether or not the bellbird was learning its song. The split in the road was where oscines and suboscines diverged from a common passerine ancestor. At that junction Kroodsma had written "90 million years ago" with a question mark after it. On the right branch of the *Y,* he'd written "songbirds." This stood for the entire lineage of oscines, all forty-five-hundred-plus species. On the left branch he had listed some common suboscine families from the neotropics: ovenbirds, woodcreepers, antbirds. Above this list, near the top of the left branch, was a second list that read "flycatchers, cotingas, tityras, manakins." This second grouping of suboscines was what interested Kroodsma. It contained both the tyrant flycatchers—which included several species that have been shown not to learn their songs—and the cotingas, the family the three-wattled bellbird belonged to. As he explained his diagram, Kroodsma noted that not only was the bellbird learning its song, but preliminary evidence indicated song-learning among some species of manakins and tityras.

This grouping of the flycatchers, cotingas, manakins, and tityras was based on a much cited study published in 1970 by Charles Sibley and Jon Ahlquist. Based on biochemical studies (analyses of egg-white proteins to be exact) of living passerines, Sibley and Ahlquist believed that these families, whose members have distinctly different outward appearances, were so closely related that the group as a whole should be considered a "superfamily," which they named the Tyrannoidea. "What really excites me," Kroodsma said, "is what this can tell us about the evolution of song-learning. We can't go back ninety million years and watch what happened when oscines and suboscines diverged, but with these bellbirds and some other closely related birds, the forces that led to their learning must be relatively recent since they diverged from a common ancestor not long ago. Maybe the social systems are the same now as they were when the learning evolved. And since not all the species in the groups seem to learn—the flycatchers for instance—it might be possible to understand the factors that have led to some learning and others not. My hunch is that it has to do with social interaction and the mating systems. If we can look long enough at this and study the bellbirds and other suboscines, we might just get some idea of how song-learning evolved."

Sibley and Ahlquist's understanding of evolutionary lineages is not universally accepted. The classification of flycatchers, cotingas, manakins, and tityras has been contested for more than a century. In fact, we have far better fossil evidence of the "first bird"—*Archaeopteryx lithographica*—from 150 million years ago than we do of any modern species of songbirds, which most believe evolved in the last few million years, possibly more recently. *Archaeopteryx lithographica* is one of the few avian fossils (one of the few fossils of *any* vertebrate) that is complete and intact–a whole animal. Alan Feduccia, an expert on avian evolution and author of *The Origin and Evolution of Birds,* notes that as "the most superb example of a specimen perfectly intermediate between two higher groups of living organisms," *Archaeopteryx lithographica* is "what has come to be called a 'missing link.'" It is such an important fossil that Feduccia calls it the "Rosetta stone of evolution."

Birds, with their fragile, lightweight bones, generally leave poor fossil records. Paleontologists typically reconstruct partial skeletons from a clavicle here, a femur there, or just as likely use a single bone as their evidence of a species' existence at a particular time. Thus, it is all the more remarkable that in 1861, just two years after Darwin published *On the Origin of Species,* a Bavarian physician who was known to trade medical services for fossils acquired a slab of limestone with the imprint of what appeared to be a reptile with wings– *Archaeopteryx lithographica.* The imprint was so detailed one could see that the wings were covered not with scales but feathers. The finely grained limestone dated from the late Mesozoic era, the age of dinosaurs, when it had been laid down in layers as the muddy sediment of a shallow sea. The fossil showed a creature the size of a crow with numerous reptilian features, including a blunt snout, reptilian teeth, and a lizardlike tail. The feathered wings, however, were clearly avian, and this flying animal had a wishbone as well, a skeletal adaptation in birds associated with flight.

Archaeopteryx lithographica illustrates the link between reptile and bird with a clarity that is missing in fossil evidence for the common ancestor of oscines and suboscines, or for that matter the ancestor of the passerines, the order of birds that now dominates the world. From caves, dried-up lakes, bogs, rock quarries, tar pits, and kitchen middens, paleontologists have unearthed the bones of ancient birds. Working from this evidence and the anatomy of living birds, they have put forth a

likely scenario for avian evolution, though not everyone inter-
prets the fossil record the same way. Great blank spots in the
record leave much to one's imagination. A controversy exists,
for instance, over whether the first birds took to flight by
gliding from perches in trees or running along the ground and
lifting off. And there is much disagreement about how to
classify some of the ancient birds. The most common theory
one is likely to come across in an ornithology textbook rests on
fossil evidence that shows that birds resembling loons, grebes,
cormorants, pelicans, flamingos, ibises, rails, and sandpipers
were present in the late Mesozoic era, the age of the dinosaurs
(245 to 66 million years ago). The cataclysmic event that
caused the extinction of the dinosaurs (an asteroid colliding
with Earth is the prevailing theory) affected most of the flora
and fauna of the time, of course, and only a few lineages of animals managed to survive into the Cenozoic era (66 million
years ago to the present) that followed. Some birds likely
made it. After this mass extinction, much of the land, water,
and air were essentially emptied of life. Notably absent were
the giant flying reptiles that had dominated the skies. Thus,
the birds that survived the cataclysm evolved rapidly to fill the
available ecological niches.

Early in the Cenozoic era, in the Eocene epoch (58–37 million years ago), many of the modern orders of birds evolved.
Large, flightless land birds, such as ostriches, existed, as did
birds of the water or water's edge (ducks and herons) and
predators of the open sky (hawks and eagles). During the
Oligocene (37–24 million years ago), climates worldwide
became drier and forests spread across the continents. In
the Miocene (24–5 million years ago), flowering plants and
insects emerged, providing niches for nectar-feeding and
insect-eating birds. This led to what is often referred to as the
"explosive radiation" of the passerines, who benefited not
only from the plants and insects that supplied them with food

but also from their ability to build nests. The latter freed them from the limited resources faced by the cavity-nesting birds that had preceded them in the forests, birds belonging to the orders Coraciiformes (kingfishers and their allies) and Piciformes (the woodpeckers and like birds).

The evolution of the passerines occurred so rapidly, relatively speaking, that distinct evolutionary lines are difficult to trace. With most other orders of birds taxonomists draw the branching schematic representation of lineages that brought *family tree* into the language. The trunk indicates the common ancestor that the birds along the branches can be traced back to. This image doesn't work for passerines. Trying to sort out which families are most closely related is troubling because the anatomy of passerines is so remarkably consistent. As a result, Alan Feduccia says, the passerine "phylogenies look like an upended head of an artist's camel hair paintbrush with myriad single strands inextricably mixed."

This is the most common picture of the timing of avian evolution, but it is not the version molecular biologists such as Sibley and Ahlquist subscribe to. Since 1970, a number of studies based not on fossils but on molecular analysis of living birds present a very different view. Two studies published in 2002, reviewed by Scott Edwards and Walter Boles in an article titled "Out of Gondwana: The origin of passerine birds," are among the most recent. Using DNA to analyze the relationships of living birds, both studies conclude that New Zealand wrens in the genus Acanthisitta are the most primitive of living passerines, placing them "at the base of the entire passerine radiation." This is significant because according to plate tectonic theory, New Zealand and Australia split from the great land mass known as Gondwana somewhere between 100 and 120 million years ago. Africa and South America, also originally sections of Gondwana, began to split apart at about the same time. If the New Zealand wrens are the most ancient passerines, then one could make the case that ancient ancestors of modern passerines existed in southern Gondwana before the continent broke up and subsequently evolved into the many modern lineages of perching birds that now cover the globe. Gondwana, according to this theory, is "the birthplace for songbirds." This theory also emphasizes that ancient passerine dispersal was successful because the birds faced no great geographic barriers as they moved outward from southern Gondwana. There was no ocean yet separating Africa and South America. Thus, even birds that were poor fliers could easily move into new areas.

Kroodsma was following this line of thinking when he wrote "90 million years ago" on the board to indicate the oscine-suboscine divergence from a common ancestor. The molecular biologists who believe in this version of events have sometimes ridiculed the old-fashioned theory of paleontologists, based on the flimsy evidence of bird bones dug out of ancient sediment. DNA is DNA, the fingerprint of a species, and one can compare fingerprints for similarities.

"The problem with this," says Alan Feduccia, "is that there just isn't any fossil evidence to support it." And it makes passerines twice as ancient (120 million years old rather than 65 million years old) as what the fossil record indicates. In other words, this means that passerines, as well as the other modern lineages of birds, were around during the time of the dinosaurs and survived the cataclysmic event that took place about 65 million years ago, causing mass extinctions of the fauna of the time. Feduccia has trouble imagining that so many small birds, "the most ecologically sensitive vertebrates," would have survived when other vertebrates did not. Moreover, Feduccia says, "there are tens of thousands of fossils from that period just before the cataclysmic event that separates the Cretaceous period from the Tertiary period, and not a single one of them is a modern bird. It boggles the mind that modern birds would have existed then but we'd find no fossils of them." As for the notion that the lack of physical boundaries made it more likely that early passerines dispersed throughout the world before Gondwana broke up, Feduccia simply points to the case of the cattle egret. An African species, the egret crossed the Atlantic and showed up in South America around 1900, then moved up and through Central America, and is now expanding its range in the southeastern United States. This happened in the span of one hundred years, nothing compared with the millions of years of geologic periods. And besides, Feduccia says, even birds that are poor fliers, such as rails, can migrate considerable distances.

Finally, Feduccia argues that fossils of passerines are virtually absent from the Northern Hemisphere until the Miocene, beginning 24 million years ago, and then in nearly every fossil deposit from that time on passerines outnumber other orders of birds by nearly ten to one. In other words, suddenly and more swiftly than any other order before them, the passerines expanded in number and diversity of species.

Still, the question remains: When and where did the order of passerines emerge? And when did the passerines split into oscines and suboscines?

"This is one of the major challenges of systematic ornithology," Feduccia says. "All we really know is that by the Miocene the passerines were the dominant bird." With respect to the question of why oscines learn their vocalizations and suboscines do not, Kroodsma could just as well have written "25 million years ago" on the board as "90 million years ago." In either case, his point would be the same: it is too difficult to trace thousands of species back along a tangle of evolutionary lines to their common ancestor and ask what happened when that ancestor evolved into two species—why did one species develop a brain that allows it to learn vocalizations and the other a brain in which the song is fixed? Too many changes have occurred since that moment so long ago to allow any reasonable speculation. But if one had two closely related species or groups of species that had recently diverged, with one lineage that learned and one that did not, fewer things would have changed since they'd diverged from a common ancestor. It might be possible to look for differences in their environment or social systems that could be correlated to vocal behavior. If some social behavior, say a particular kind of breeding system, appeared to be directly correlated to song-learning, then it was possible to at least make an educated guess that this had something to do with the different vocal abilities of oscines and suboscines. Kroodsma admits he is uncomfortable with the number of uncertainties involved in this, and the conflicting accounts of avian evolution only add to the sense that he is standing on shifting sands. He knows he is reaching for some invisible but conceivable moment that took place somewhere along a half-imagined road in time.

Muddy roads were our problem on the second day of recording. Weather was always a concern. Not long after dark on our first night, it began to rain. A soft shower turned into a hard, steady rain, which continued throughout the night. When I rose at four-thirty, Kroodsma was already awake. He had woken up throughout the night and looked out the window to check how hard it was raining. Now, in the early light, it was still raining steadily. Kroodsma thought it was best to eat and get ready to go out in case the weather broke just after sunrise, but half an hour later the ridge was still engulfed in a dark cloud. He'd planned on recording at Stuckey's farm, but now he paced a bit, then made up his mind to abandon the idea. Stuckey's was on the other side of Monteverde and we could lose an hour or more just going there and back if it was raining there as well. It was better to stay right here and record nearby if the rain broke. Yesterday afternoon Kroodsma had spotted a banded bellbird along the entrance road to the station. It wouldn't be unusual for it to rain for an hour or two more, then clear for half an hour, then rain again. If the rain stopped for even half an hour, he could make the walk in a matter of minutes and record that bird. And of course Finca Las Americas was only a couple of hundred yards to the north. Kroodsma took advantage of the downtime to type up his notes from yesterday.

By seven-thirty the dark cloud hanging over the ridge began to lighten. Now it was a thick mist. The rain stopped for a few minutes, then started up again. Finally, by nine the rain stopped long enough to get Kroodsma's attention. Julio came out onto the covered porch where Kroodsma was looking at the sky. "Let's go," Kroodsma said.

Julio looked again at the clouds, shaking his head for effect. "My parabola is clean enough. I don't need to wash it."

"Well, I'm going to record at Finca Las Americas," Kroodsma said. "You could go across the road to Arce's farm and look for banded birds there." Julio could not seem to think of what to say. He walked off toward his room as Kroodsma turned and went to collect his recording equipment. When Kroodsma returned, Julio had only his binoculars with him.

"I'll look at Arce's to see what is there," Julio said. "Maybe I'll see some blue sky too. Then I can come back and get my recorder." Julio tended to be more cautious with his equipment than Kroodsma, no doubt because it was harder to come by. The parabola he was carrying was once Kroodsma's. Julio had been recording with a shotgun microphone, but when Kroodsma loaned him a parabola so he could hear the difference, Julio was so delighted Kroodsma insisted he keep it.

Danilo, ever faithful, arrived this morning despite the downpour. He and Kroodsma walked down the entrance road to the stand of trees less than a hundred yards from the station, where yesterday afternoon Kroodsma had seen the banded bird. The group of trees, which edged up to the entrance road, was a tiny island of the forest that was here before the land was cleared. It was one of the islands of remnant forest we would often work in throughout our stay in

Monteverde. But none were as small as this. We could walk around it in four or five minutes without hurrying. Still, the trees were tall and leafy, the undergrowth dense, and the island was just big enough that the bellbird we heard calling from somewhere near the center was hidden from our view. Kroodsma stopped and listened. Danilo put down his tripod a moment and listened as well. "It is Rojo/Plata, I think," Danilo said. "This is where he was." Danilo had seen a banded bird–Rojo/Plata–Rojo/Plata–in these same trees last week during the census. And that was the band combination Kroodsma thought he'd seen yesterday on a bird in these trees.

"Do you see him?" Kroodsma asked.

"He is in the other side, I think." And with that Danilo picked up his tripod and began walking slowly along the edge of the trees. If a bellbird was nearby, Kroodsma and Danilo spoke in short, half-whispered sentences, when they spoke at all. All movement was purposeful and slow. Kroodsma held his parabola in the general direction of the calling bellbird and looked down at the VU meter on the recorder at his side. Seconds later the bellbird fell silent. Kroodsma waited. After several minutes of silence we walked around the trees to find Danilo, who had not gotten a sight line on the bird, but thought he saw him fly off. "I think it *must* be Rojo/Plata," Danilo said.

"Yes, but it would be nice to see those bands clearly." Kroodsma was already turning his attention to another bird a couple of hundred yards to the north, this one a Talamanca singer. The *quack* from the Talamanca singers is almost cartoonish. One imagines a bellbird with a sore throat. Sometimes the Talamanca song begins with two *quack*s, sometimes three, and there are no whistles. This bird was high in a tree on the far edge of a field, too far to get a good recording. Kroodsma turned on his tape recorder anyway to get something before

202

we tried to move closer. Danilo moved into the field a short distance, set his tripod down, and leveled the legs. Before he could get the scope trained on the bird, we heard a second bird, a Monteverde singer, calling from nearby in the same tree. Kroodsma continued recording for a few minutes, then stopped.

"Do you see the second bird?"

"Maybe it is Rojo/Plata," Danilo said, still trying to find the birds in his scope. "Oh, I see the Talamanca bird. He is sixth-year, I think. Almost white."

Kroodsma began recording again, picking up both the Monteverde and Talamanca calls.

"Don, I think this is one bird," Danilo said. Now the scope was focused on the bird and Danilo was studying it. "But he is sixth-year. Yes. He's sixth-year."

Kroodsma stopped recording and scanned the far trees with his binoculars, and he too could see only one bird. "Is there another bird in the trees behind him?"

"No. Just one bird. I think he is making both calls. Oh, he flew. He's gone."

Kroodsma was both excited and surprised. The oldest bilingual singer he had ever come across was a fourth-year bird, and Kroodsma speculated that the young birds were trying out both dialects, then choosing one of them as an adult, which, if plumage was any indication, occurred by the seventh year. But this bird was nearly an adult already. "What could this mean?" Kroodsma asked, leaving the question in the air. Kroodsma continued to think aloud, as he so often did when he didn't understand something: "This is what some of the guides have told us, that there are some older bilingual singers, but I'd never heard one. I doubted them. I guess I shouldn't have, but all the bilingual birds we have seen have been juveniles, and it just made sense that juvenile birds were experimenting with the two different dialects. Or"–now Kroodsma laughed lightly at himself—"it made sense *to me* anyway. Who knows what the bellbirds think of it." Kroodsma looked one more time at the now empty trees in the distance. "I wish I had gotten a better recording. I was too far away."

"Maybe he will come back," Danilo said.

"We have to get more recordings of him. *We just have to.*" Then Kroodsma wondered aloud again if a second bird was calling directly behind the first one, hidden from our view, but none of us saw a second bird, nor did a second bird fly off when the calling stopped.

Kroodsma could not dwell on these thoughts because now another bellbird started singing, this one clearly visible, though also more than a hundred yards away. And it was banded.

"I think it is Rojo/Plata–Rojo/Plata," Danilo said hopefully. "I can see rojo-plata on the left leg pretty good." It was the bird we had been looking for only moments earlier in the patch of trees along the entrance road. We had wandered off the road into a coffee plantation to the north, beyond which lay the small clearing at Finca Las Americas that Kroodsma had dubbed "the black hole of bellbirds" in 1999. Walking in between the rows of trees, Kroodsma drew closer to the bird. I looked through my binoculars, hoping to see the bands. Suddenly, a second bird landed on the same branch as rojo-plata. Rojo-plata, who was near the end of the exposed branch, jerked upward and leapfrogged back over the intruder, taking a place on the inside. The move was quick and precise, a practiced motion, it seemed. Now rojo-plata began sidling down the branch toward the intruder. He shouldered up against him and began edging him toward the end of the branch, as if it were a gangplank. When the intruder had been driven to the very end of the branch, he leaned out into thin air, clinging to his last inch of tree, trying not to fall. Rojo-plata leaned with him, shoulder to shoulder, opened his beak wide, put it to the intruder's ear, and began gulping down air. Seconds later, rojo-plata delivered a thunderclap of a *bonk* into the intruder's ear, which sent him tumbling off the end of the branch like a reluctant skydiver.

This was the three-wattled bellbird's "changing places display," a routine that seemed to come straight out of avian vaudeville. It was a wonder that bellbirds weren't rendered deaf by it, but the birds who take the abuse come back for more. Rojo-plata's intruder returned immediately to the inside of the branch, and rojo-plata repeated the maneuver. This went on for several minutes. Usually the "intruder" was a juvenile, and Kroodsma thought the actions might have something to do with the young bird listening to the adult, his ear almost in the adult's mouth while it prepared to *bonk*. The swishing sounds in the bellbird's call are soft and barely audible. Kroodsma can hear them only with the parabolic microphone focused exactly on the bird. Was some kind of training going on here? Was the young bird learning how to work the muscles to vocalize properly?

A short while later dark clouds rolled into the area and a mist covered everything. The bellbirds looked like ghostly figures in the trees. Kroodsma already had a garbage bag covering his backpack, and now he pulled out a second bag and used it to cover the parabola and recorder. He then put a large green poncho over his head and covered everything. Rain fell suddenly, steady but moderate. We stood beneath the trees at the margin of the clearing, trying to decide if we should wait this rain shower out or head back to the station before it stormed harder. Within twenty minutes it was raining harder and the skies darkened, so Kroodsma reluctantly set off for the conservation center, and just in time. As we got to the porch, lightning split the sky and it began to pour.

This ninety minutes of recording in between showers was it

for the day. Kroodsma stored his equipment and went back to typing up his notes.

Rojo-plata was still on Kroodsma's mind the next day, as was the mysterious sixth-year bilingual bird. The skies were gray again so it seemed best to stay close to home. Kroodsma was not entirely satisfied with the looks Danilo had gotten at rojo-plata's bands. He wanted to confirm them. Shortly after sunrise we were back at the little island of trees near the entrance road. Danilo was optimistic that we would find Rojo/Plata–Rojo/Plata in the vicinity again today. "And maybe the sixth-year bilingual too," he said to Kroodsma. But the early morning passed without any bilingual birds. We wandered from one area of Finca Las Americas to another, and though Kroodsma recorded two banded birds, neither was rojo-plata. If the sixth-year bilingual bird was using this area, we would likely have heard him. Kroodsma tried to reconcile himself to the idea that the bird was just passing through yesterday and we would not see or hear him again. Finally, late in the morning, back at the small island of trees, we heard a bellbird calling in roughly the same place as yesterday. Danilo, without a word, set off around the far edge while Kroodsma recorded a few minutes from the entrance road. When we followed Danilo's path, we found him hunched over, looking through the scope.

"He's facing this way. I see the bands," Danilo whispered. Kroodsma nodded without answering, and turned the recorder on immediately. The bellbird continued calling loudly, occasionally changing positions on the branch so that he faced away from us, but after several minutes Kroodsma had some good recordings.

"Can you see the bands clearly?" Kroodsma asked.

"Yes. He's in the sun." But then Danilo asked me to look

through the scope. I looked, expecting to see two identical bands, red over silver, but instead the band combination was Rojo/Plata–Rojo/Verde. When I said this, Danilo was relieved. "Yes. It's not Rojo/Plata–Rojo/Plata. He has green on the right leg. But I saw Rojo/Plata–Rojo/Plata here on the census."

"Were you sure?" Kroodsma asked.

"Yes. But now I wonder."

"Did different people on different days see the band combination wrong, and see it wrong several times?" Kroodsma was thinking aloud again. "And really it was Rojo/Verde all along? Or could there be another bird in this same area with such a similar band combination? Well, that doesn't seem likely, does it? One would like to know for sure–to see both of these birds with the two different bands and not have any doubt."

All of us looked again through the scope. The band combination, in good light, was unmistakable: Rojo/Plata–Rojo/Verde. And this bird was in its sixth year, the same age as the bird earlier identified, on the census and by Kroodsma two days ago, as Rojo/Plata–Rojo/Plata. This made the odds longer–that there were two different birds of the same age with similar band combinations using the same small island of trees. Kroodsma decided that we must have seen the bands incorrectly all along, something that would be borne out much later with detailed analysis of sonograms of this bird. Kroodsma's impulse to record at every opportunity and look and look again at band combinations served him well. It had taken two days to be certain of the bands on this one bird, but this accuracy is exactly why Kroodsma's work is so highly regarded.

Yesterday as we were listening to Rojo/Plata–Rojo/Verde, Danilo bent down and picked up a hard, green fruit not much larger than an acorn. "Lauraceae," he said, handing it to me. It was the bellbird's favorite food, a small wild avocado produced by trees in the Lauraceae family. According to one study, nearly half of the fruit the three-wattled bellbird eats in the Monteverde area comes from one or another species of Lauraceae trees. All four species of bellbirds are frugivores, and their subsistence on fruit is linked to their origin as a genus.

Whether the oscine-suboscine split occurred 90 million years ago or 25 million years ago, both lineages appear to have spread north from Australia and New Zealand into what is now the Old World. There, the oscines became the dominant passerines while the suboscines moved from Africa into South America, which became their stronghold. Today, nearly a thousand species of suboscines are found in South and Central America while less than fifty occur in the Old World. After South America broke off from Gondwana roughly 110 million years ago, it drifted slowly westward, a massive, isolated island-continent. For much of its 100-million-year journey to its present location the land was predominantly low-lying forest with a tropical climate. The few species of suboscines that had originally inhabited the continent split and split again, radiating into every available ecological niche. Woodcreepers, ovenbirds, and antbirds—grouped into a superfamily known as Furnarioidea—foraged on the ground and undergrowth, gleaning insects from branches and twigs, while the flycatchers, cotingas, manakins, sharpbills, and plant cutters—the Tyrannoidea superfamily—fed on insects or fruit, generally plucking them from the air in flight. Of the former group, flycatchers specialized in insects, manakins in small fruits of the forest understory, and cotingas in larger understory fruits.

The bird life of Central America was developing at the same time. The northern half of the region has existed for approximately 60 million years as a southern peninsula of the North American continent, while the southern portion of Central America—Costa Rica and Panama—emerged first as volcanic islands 50 million years ago. Early on, the chain of islands likely became home to land birds that typically colonize islands—herons, hawks, pigeons, parrots, kingfishers, and waterfowl. A few other birds may have used the islands to expand north or south, thrushes and jays perhaps crossing from North to South America, and flycatchers and hummingbirds moving in the opposite direction. By the time ocean levels fell 3 to 5 million years ago and the islands became a continuous, slender piece of geographic cartilage connecting North and South America, bird life in the area was already well established.

The bellbird, however, would be a late arrival to Costa Rica, as would members of the cotinga family in general. The cotingas appear to have evolved entirely in South America and then spread into Central America when the land bridge was complete. As evidence, ornithologists note that there are no genera of cotingas endemic to Central America, as one would expect if some members of the family evolved there, nor are there any great differences between species within a genus. With sixty-five species, the cotingas are a very successful lineage of sub-oscines. And a colorful and strange one. Among passerines they are second only to the birds of paradise in their orna-mentation, says David Snow, who has written the authoritative book on the Cotingidae. Some cotingas are royal blue head to toe with purple patches on their throat. Some are parrot-green with black heads and bright yellow bibs. The "red cotingas" are scarlet and black. A few species are snowy white. Some have long forked tails, and several species have crests, including the umbrella birds with their spectacular mops of feathers and the bizarre-looking cocks of the rock, whose top-heavy crests (brilliant orange!) are stranger than the headgear of the guards at Buckingham Palace. Given a picture of a three-wattled bellbird, with its striking coloration and dan-gling wattles, even a child might guess it belonged among the cotingas.

Yet the bellbirds are so distinct that it is difficult to tell which other cotingas they are most closely related to. The bell-bird skull and syrinx are the most highly modified of any species in the family, the former to accommodate the bellbird's extraordinarily wide gape, an adaptation for fruit-eating. It is also difficult to determine when the common ancestor of the bellbird originated, though given the bellbirds' reliance on fruit and their distribution—all four species breed in mountain forests—it is likely they evolved to take advantage of fruit-bearing trees that populated the new habitat of mountain ranges that rose from the lowland forests. Judging by distri-bution patterns and morphology of the current species, it appears that the first bellbird originated in the forests of the Guiana Shield or in eastern Brazil. At some point, this species split into eastern and western forms, and those two forms each split once again. The eastern form yielded the bearded and bare-throated bellbirds, both of which share many traits, most noticeably a fleshy throat. The western form became the white and three-wattled bellbirds, each having a long wattle hanging from the top of the upper mandible (complemented of course by two more wattles in the case of the latter).

The current range of the white bellbird extends throughout much of Venezuela and Guyana. From there, long-ago members of this species moved westward, wandering eventually as far as Nicaragua. Later, cut off from the original population of white bellbirds, these wanderers became the stock from which the three-wattled bellbird evolved. The three-wattled bellbird's journey across time and space most likely was accompanied by Lauraceae trees. A widespread family throughout the New World tropics, Lauraceae is a dominant tree in the Monteverde area, and it's not far-fetched to say that their success in spreading throughout the forest is directly linked to the three-wattled bellbird. As much as the bellbirds depend on the Lauraceae, the Lauraceae in turn depend on the bellbirds, which regurgitate the seeds after eating the fruit, in effect planting more Lauraceae trees in the forest. This kind of interdependence between fruit-eating birds and fruit-bearing trees is not unusual, but the three-wattled bellbird, unique in so many ways, is also uniquely effective as a seed disperser.

The bellbird moves back and forth from one favorite perch to another throughout the day, feeding occasionally on the fruit of the Lauraceae trees as it does. Consequently, the bellbird takes the fruit away from the "parent" tree, thereby spreading the Lauraceae seeds throughout the forest. Furthermore, the bellbird is picky about the kind of perch it favors. The perch is nearly always a broken-off branch with few or no leaves. Thus, sunlight penetrates the forest through this opening in the vegetation, shining on the ground below where the regurgitated seeds have fallen. The sunshine not only increases the likelihood the seeds will germinate, but also reduces fungal pathogens that destroy them. There is one minor imperfection in this mutually beneficial relationship.

Getting to the fruit is not easy for such a large, heavy bird. The bellbirds find it difficult to work their way to the end of branches where the fruit hangs, so they must often dangle precariously from a branch swaying under their weight. They may hang upside down, flapping their wings for stability as they pull off the fruit. More striking, they will sometimes pluck fruit on the wing, as most other cotingas do, snatching the avocado from the branch as they fly by, though the bird may have to make several flybys before it meets its target perfectly. Barbara Snow (David Snow's wife), who studied bellbirds in Monteverde in the 1970s, once saw a bellbird misjudge the ripeness of a fruit. The avocado did not snap off when the bellbird grabbed it, leaving the bird, a victim of whiplash, hanging momentarily by its beak.

The lumber of Lauraceae trees is used in construction and furniture, and the bellbird's population decline is almost certainly linked to deforestation. If the bellbird is lost, one can speculate that the forests as they now exist will be lost as well. Hoping never to face this scenario, Debra Hamilton has launched a campaign to plant Lauraceae trees throughout the Monteverde area, a project most farmers have embraced. The Lauraceae's large, spreading crowns make them good shade trees. Thousands of seedlings, nurtured by local volunteers, were planted in recent years. Whether this will counterbalance the general deforestation is impossible to say, but the effort is admirable.

The irony is that deforestation makes it easier for Kroodsma to locate bellbirds in the remnant forests with Lauraceae trees. Throughout our stay in Monteverde, it seemed odd that it was so easy to find such a wild bird. And the bellbird is indeed a wild and wary creature, not a cooperative subject for study. To capture the bellbirds for banding, Hamilton has to raise a mist net off the ground for the high-flying birds and rig a system of ropes that allows her to lower the net quickly once a bellbird is caught. Caught in a mist net, many species of birds will struggle for a few seconds, then give up and hang silently like a shuttlecock, but the bellbird is outraged when trapped in a net. George Powell learned early on that the birds struggle so much and scream with such force that they wear themselves out. Powell had to take several home with him and nurse them back to health after they overworked their respiratory systems screeching at the indignity of their situation. After a few such experiences, Powell and Hamilton began sedating them. Having watched Hamilton capture the bellbirds in 1999, it was hard to imagine them in cages in a laboratory. Wild as tigers, the bellbirds are the polar opposites of cooperative zebra finches.

Half of our week in Costa Rica was behind us already. Kroodsma had recordings of five banded bellbirds, and the remainder of the week would be spent trying to track down more of the banded birds from the census. The days assumed a familiar shape. We went from one site to another; Julio headed off in one direction and Kroodsma and Danilo in another. The repetitiveness of the work would have made it dull if it weren't for the bellbird, which I never grew tired of watching. Even so, hours often went by slowly. Occasionally part of me longed for some adventure, perhaps a long trek up a steep mountainside to some spot in the cloud forest where a particular bellbird held the key to Kroodsma's research. If the journey was difficult and we faced moderate danger, all the better. If the bird was elusive, appearing only after hours of searching, better yet.

Instead, we continued to work on farms, skirting the edges of pastures as we listened for bellbirds, and slipping into the forest along trails for an hour or two at a time. Stepping over electrified fences, unsure if we could clear the top wire, was as close as we got to high drama. And our adventures more likely involved cows than wild animals. For Stuckey's farm, where we spent the fourth day of recording, we wore high rubber boots, expecting to encounter some rain-soaked paths, and it was a good thing.

In midmorning we found ourselves confronted with a low-lying stretch of muddy road bordered closely by forest on each side. The cows must have passed this way each day, and apparently something about the spot stimulated them, because for a hundred feet the road became a trough of mud and manure. The earthy mixture rose above the ankle. We sloshed through it, trying to find solid footing as we went. Slick rocks below the surface threw us off-balance. "Not a good place to fall down," Kroodsma said. With that picture in mind I imagined Kroodsma explaining to Greg Budney why the loaned Portadat recorder had a pastoral odor. Halfway through the narrows, Kroodsma stopped. He heard a bellbird nearby. He steadied himself, lifted the parabola toward the bird, and turned on the recorder. We waited, holding our positions carefully. Like toy figures on plastic bases, our feet seemed to merge into the muck below. Moments later the scene grew livelier when we were met by a herd of cows coming from the other direction. There was nowhere to go so we stood as the cows flowed around us, brushing us as they went. Most ignored their obstacle, but a few eyed us suspiciously. One curious animal stopped to sniff Danilo's scope. "Go," Danilo said, waving his arm, "get away," and the cow took a couple of quick steps, then resumed her easy gait toward the familiar pasture up ahead.

At Stuckey's farm we saw banded birds but were not able to identify them, so Kroodsma ended the day with more samples of the kinds of recordings he already had. The next day, a bit tired of the routine, I decided to spend some time on my own at Finca Las Americas while Kroodsma and Danilo drove north of Monteverde where three banded birds had been spotted on the census. For the first time all week it didn't rain, so Kroodsma stayed out until late afternoon. When he returned, he had a big smile on his face. "We got the big one today," he said. "We found only one of the banded birds, but the one we got was the important one."

Kroodsma and Danilo had come across Plata/Rojo–Plata/ Rojo, a mature adult that was singing mainly Talamanca songs, but appeared to be trying out Monteverde sounds too, "as if he was taking up Monteverde as a second language," Kroodsma said. Two years ago, Julio recorded this bird in the same area. It was already an adult then, a Talamanca singer, so now it seemed to be changing its song, further proof that the bellbirds learn their vocalizations. This was the kind of dramatic moment I was still half-expecting despite knowing that fieldwork rarely yields such moments. I had chosen the wrong morning to stay at the conservation center. Each day, Kroodsma said the same thing as he trudged off to record just one more bird: "You never know which bird is going to tell you what you want to know." Now, here was a bilingual adult bird, and better yet it was banded and had been recorded once before. We hadn't climbed a mountain to find it, but Kroodsma was excited.

I waited on the porch while Kroodsma took his equipment inside. When he came back out a few minutes later, he was shaking his head slowly from side to side. He looked at the ground for a minute, then raised his head. "I think I spoke too soon," he said. "Now I remember that Julio didn't get any recordings of the bird in 1999. There were some chain saws in the background and he didn't want to waste tape. He told me about the vocalizations; I remember that. Well, it's still important. It would be better if we had recordings from two years ago, but if he is bilingual as an adult, it tells us something important." The bilingual bellbirds are some of the strongest evidence Kroodsma has to support his claim that bellbirds learn to sing. This is oscine, not suboscine, behavior. Young songbirds exposed to two different dialects often sing a little of each dialect. The white-crowned sparrows Marler and others have studied so carefully are a perfect example. A fledgling white-crown that lives near a dialect boundary will learn songs from both dialects, then as an adult choose one or the other or sing both. Kroodsma has now recorded numerous juvenile bellbirds that use both Talamanca and Monteverde vocalizations. If the Monteverde and Talamanca bellbirds were two species whose songs were encoded in their genes, the birds near the boundary between populations would be singing hybrid songs—neither *bonk*s nor *quack*s, but something in between. But the bilingual singers are using notes from each dialect just as song-learning songbirds at dialect boundaries do.

Lost momentarily in Kroodsma's talk of the adult bilingual singer was some bad news. In pursuit of another banded bird, Danilo had stumbled into a thorn tree. A thorn had lodged itself deep in his shin. Because Danilo had not yet gotten a good look at the banded bellbird, he insisted he could walk a while longer. By the time Kroodsma called off the search and took Danilo to a clinic, the thorn had worked its way well below the surface of his skin. The doctor, who appeared to have even less skill than he had concern for Danilo's pain, gave up trying to extract the thorn intact and broke it off, leaving half of it where it was lodged—but not before he had made several crude incisions. Danilo was limping badly by the time Kroodsma got him home.

The next morning Kroodsma headed back to the farm where he and Danilo had spotted the bilingual adult. Yesterday, the bird had moved back and forth between several tall trees, so Kroodsma and Julio entered a pasture on a hillside midway between the perches and sat down in the grass to wait. Because the trees were several hundred yards apart Kroodsma brought a thirty-six-inch, tripod-mounted parabola, a large enough reflector to get a good recording even if the bird appeared only briefly in one of the far trees. Half an hour after sunrise, there was still no sign of the bellbird. We waited in the pasture for another hour and a half. The bilingual sixth-year bird we had seen briefly several days ago never reappeared, and now this bilingual adult was proving elusive too.

"Time to give up," Kroodsma said, and with that we headed to Stuckey's farm. On the way, we stopped by the roadside to meet another of the area's guides, who was to take Danilo's place. The morning's bad luck continued: our guide never showed up. And so the morning went. Shortly before noon Kroodsma stood by the car thinking he was reaching a point of diminishing returns. "We've probably already learned about 90 percent of what we can on this trip about the bell-bird's vocalizations," he said. "Tomorrow is our last day. What is the wisest way to use the little time we have left here? I'd like to go back to Arce's farm and try to see the bands on that bird Danilo was following when he ran into the thorn, and we should probably go back to Santa Elena again tomorrow morning to see if that bilingual adult shows up."

W hy does the bellbird learn its vocalizations when other closely related suboscines do not? The answer, Kroodsma thought, must have something to do with the three-wattled bellbird's social system, in particular its breeding behavior. In 1974, Barbara Snow spent nearly two months in Monteverde watching a group of male bellbirds during the breeding season. Her study provided the foundation upon which George Powell and Debra Hamilton built their ongoing research, which in turn underlies Kroodsma's work. Barbara Snow's observations would eventually be a key element in Kroodsma's understanding of why bellbirds learn. In April of 1974, Barbara Snow staked out an area in the mountains that measured 1,400 by 3,200 meters, some of it in virgin forest, some forest that bordered cleared farmland. Each day for seven and a half weeks she watched thirteen adult male bellbirds as they called from favored perches within their territories. The birds were extremely vocal, calling an average of 83 percent to 93 percent of the daylight hours, three times per minute, two thousand calls per day.

The territories varied in size. One bird occupied an area of 30 by 70 meters, another a much larger holding of 50 by 450 meters. All the birds were choosy when it came to one particular aspect of their real estate. They required two kinds of perches to call from, one of them a "high calling post" in an emergent tree that gave them a view of the forest from above the canopy. The high calling post, almost always a broken-off dead branch, was often in a tree on the edge of a steep valley or on the edge of land cleared for a farm. Either perch gave males a particularly good view of approaching females, since bellbirds frequently fly above the canopy of the forest. The other perch, below the canopy level, was reserved for interaction with other bellbirds that entered their territory, a "visiting perch" Barbara Snow called it. The visiting perch had even stricter requirements. Typically, it too was a dead branch, and it was positioned in a gap where light entered the forest, the result usually of a fallen tree. Snow measured twelve of the visiting perches, which were ten to twenty-two meters above the ground. Their diameter was twenty-five to fifty millimeters, and the last forty-five to sixty centimeters of the branch was bare of other side branches. Furthermore, they rose slightly upward from the horizontal, usually ten to fifteen degrees. The conditions of the branches were necessitated by the bellbird's elaborate courtship displays.

Snow documented three different kinds of displays. If a female bellbird flew into a male's territory, the male often responded with a "flight display," which involved leaving his perch and flying to another nearby branch, three to five meters away. There he crouched and fanned his tail, then returned to the original perch and assumed the same crouched, fan-tailed position. Often a female would approach, landing on a branch just above a male. This inspired a "wattle shaking" display. The male, crouching again, looked down and shook his wattles back and forth, then looked up at the female above him. He appeared to be "bowing" to the female, Barbara Snow remarked. The male would repeat this action, sometimes making "small, quick, sideways hops" along the perch in between the wattle shaking. If the female joined the male on the high calling post, he might fly down to the visiting perch, and if she followed, the male engaged in more wattle shaking. This might also lead to the "changing places" display, which I had seen a few days ago—"ordeal by sound," Snow called it. Snow watched these displays many times over. Though she never saw them lead to mating, she had seen similar displays by the white and bearded bellbirds and had witnessed mating of the latter.

These stereotyped displays are not typical avian mating behavior. Moreover, Snow saw not only females visit the thirteen males, but also immature males and some adult males as well. And both led to the same behavior. The bellbirds were not singing to defend a territory from other males, nor were they interested in forming a pair bond with one female to mate and raise young. Most birds—90 percent is the current estimate—pool their resources and energy by raising their offspring together, the best way to ensure their reproductive success (though recent studies have shown that "extrapair mating" occurs quite often among some species in these seemingly "monogamous" relationships). In a few species, the male mates with more than one female (known as polygyny). Though the female raises the young alone, she benefits, the current thinking goes, by mating with an experienced, successful male who has chosen a prime territory rich in resources. There are also species in which a single female mates with several males, polyandry.

The bellbird's mating system belonged to a fourth category. Each male bellbird appeared to attract an indefinite number of female visitors, likely mating with any female he could impress with the flair of his wattle shaking, the precision of his flight display, the intensity of his changing-places maneuver. Biologists call this for what it is: promiscuity, an "indiscriminate, casual sexual relationship, usually of brief duration," according to

Frank Gill in his well-known text, *Ornithology*. Furthermore, some promiscuous species display in communal arenas, or "leks," chosen for that purpose only. In North America, for instance, male sage grouse gather in leks to perform. They strut about, tails spread into spike-tipped fans and their chests puffed out, revealing the special yellow air sacs they inflate and deflate to create a popping sound. A lek may contain seventy or more male birds, though the male at the center of the arena is dominant, around whom the hierarchy descends. The intense competition has major consequences because females choose their mate based on the hierarchy, which means only a few males will mate. Studies indicate that less than 10 percent of males in large leks achieve 70–80 percent of all the mating.

In such a scenario, the younger, less experienced males no doubt pay close attention to the actions of the successful males. These close-quarter encounters, mixed with the great drive to mate, have surely led to the elaborate displays that are part circus high-wire act, part Greek drama. Some species of manakins hop and flip about as if jerked by invisible strings. The white-bearded manakin at one point in his display appears to slide down a vertical branch like a firefighter going down a pole. Groups of swallow-tailed manakins, lined up shoulder to shoulder on a branch, leap over each other in a synchronized motion that looks like a turning wheel. Species such as manakins and cotingas are more likely to display in leks, many believe, because they are fruit eaters, and fruit is a reliable, readily available source of food to a female raising young on her own. The same is true for nectar-feeding birds, which may explain why several species of hummingbirds display in leks.

There is considerable debate about why the lek system evolved at all, and what evolutionary advantages it provides. One theory posits that males distracted by their courtship displays are less likely to be surprised by a predator if many males are grouped together. Frank Gill observes that "clustering of males on leks is partly a natural consequence of the tendency of young, inexperienced males to gather near older or successful males." The most discussed theories, though, involve the opportunity this provides for females to compare one male with another and choose the male who sustains the display most effectively. A few studies indicate this may reflect the bird's general health. Thus, a female chooses the healthiest bird with the best genes to pass on to her young.

The three-wattled bellbirds are spread too far apart during the breeding season to be considered a classic lek-displaying species, but their loose clustering, called an exploded lek, is actually more common than conventional leks. Frank Gill, considering why this system is more numerous, points out that "failure to consummate copulations because of disruption is one of the major liabilities of joining an aggregation of eager males." Therefore, "the advantages of dispersed display with little disruption counter the potential advantages of displaying together." The female bellbirds, perhaps, have the best of both worlds. "This intense competition to impress the females *must* have something to do with why the bellbirds learn their vocalizations," Kroodsma says. "How else could you explain it?"

On the final day in Monteverde, Kroodsma and Julio split up, each returning to sites where they recorded banded birds earlier. They also made one last futile attempt to find the bilingual adult north of Santa Elena. Despite some bad luck during the last couple of days, Kroodsma ended the week in Monteverde with 142 individual recordings that filled up six cassette tapes. His observations would later yield forty-two single-spaced pages of notes. He would need to review the recordings carefully before determining how many different birds he had recorded, but it appeared to be four dozen or more. He and Danilo confirmed the bands on seven birds, and he had recordings of every permutation of a bellbird song he knew of: juvenile birds of various ages with undeveloped songs, juvenile bilingual singers, adults of both the Monteverde and Talamanca dialects, and, of course, brief recordings of the sixth-year and the adult bilingual birds. Some of the recordings were not high quality, but many were excellent. Despite the rain, he had plenty of data.

In the evening, Kroodsma called Danilo to say farewell and was surprised to hear him insist that his leg was feeling much better after two days of rest. He wanted to go to Nicaragua. Given the uncertainty of finding bellbirds there, Kroodsma was happy to have Danilo's help. Our plan was to take a late-afternoon flight the following day from San José to Managua. Although we could have driven the two hundred miles, we were warned against it. A biologist who had worked in Nicaragua told Kroodsma the highway border guards might be difficult to deal with, especially if they noticed the recording equipment. She also thought it was unwise for us to be traveling in Nicaragua without a Nicaraguan guide. The government was stable, but poverty was severe in places, in particular in the countryside. One pair of our binoculars cost more than many people made in a year. With this in mind, Kroodsma decided to leave the recordings he had made, the Portadat recorder, and anything else irreplaceable at Julio's house in San José. The trip was filled with uncertainties. All we knew was that a coffee farmer, Victor Janovich, would send someone to meet us at the Managua airport. From there we'd go north to his farm near Matagalpa, where we should find bellbirds. This much Julio had arranged through a Nicaraguan biologist he'd met at a conference. In addition, two of the biologist's students would accompany us in search of bellbirds. They were to meet us at the airport, as would Danilo, who had chosen a less expensive but bumpier route from Monteverde to Managua—a ten-hour bus ride.

Early the following morning, we rose in darkness, loaded our gear into the small rented Toyota, and crammed ourselves in. Danilo had to catch a bus on the main highway at 8 A.M., so we had one extra person in the car on the way down the mountain, and thus less space for luggage. We wedged bags into the spaces around our feet and balanced others on our knees. Kroodsma, whose six-foot-two-inch frame already gave him little elbow room, stuck the Portadat recorder in his lap, where the steering wheel cleared it by only an inch or two. It was awkward, but Kroodsma was concerned about how much jostling the recorder would take on the ride ahead. We had only two hours to get down the mountain to the bus stop. Although the rocky mountain road had been graded a few days earlier—a once-a-year event, Danilo said—it was still not much smoother than a gravel pit in places. Kroodsma hunched over the steering wheel and took to the challenge. We slid and bounced around curves, all of us holding on to some part of the car frame as we went, arriving at the highway with several minutes to spare.

From there we drove to Julio's house, stored some of our valuables, and, after a leisurely lunch, made our way back through the clotted San José traffic to the airport for our 5 P.M. flight. Kroodsma's plans called for four full days in Nicaragua, then a return to San José on the fifth day to catch an evening flight to the United States. It was not much time considering how little we knew about the Nicaraguan bellbirds and their whereabouts, but Kroodsma felt that whatever he learned about these birds was a bonus. As much as he hoped to hear what they sounded like, his research did not depend on it.

We touched down in Managua at dusk. Although there was no reason to be concerned about our safety, we hoped not to be detained and questioned about the recording equipment. Parabolic reflectors are generally difficult to pack and tend to be conspicuous, but one company makes a reflector of soft, clear plastic. It can, in fact, be rolled up, which is what Kroodsma did. He kept it inside a rain poncho tucked under his arm as we proceeded through customs. Outside in the warm night air we found Danilo and seconds later were approached by a man who introduced himself as Javier, the driver Victor Janovich had sent for us. Two nights earlier, however, when Kroodsma had talked to Janovich, he'd assured Kroodsma he would send two vehicles since, counting the two Nicaraguan students, there were six of us. Javier knew nothing more than that he was to pick us up and drive us to Matagalpa. Then again, there was no sign of the two Nicaraguan biology students. Since we had been traveling for twelve hours already, no one wanted to wait to see if two more people showed up, then try to figure out who was going to sit in whose lap. In a white Ford Explorer, we drove off, heading north into the dark countryside past small fires where the day's garbage burned, attended by children and dogs. Now and then men and women walking on the shoulder of the highway turned to look with blank faces at the large, white SUV as we passed.

In Matagalpa, a small, dusty town, Javier took us to Victor Janovich's office, a nondescript building on a side street. There Julio made a phone call to see what had happened to the two students. I was happy to get out of the car, but as Kroodsma, Julio, and Danilo walked toward the building with Javier leading the way, I realized the keys were in the ignition and several windows were rolled down. "I'll wait here," I said.

Javier turned and motioned to me. "It's okay. It's safe." Across the darkened street was a brightly lit Toyota dealership where two guards armed with shotguns were talking. I leaned against the car. "I'll just stay here," I said. The buildings along the street were unadorned stucco painted a mustard yellow. There were no windows at street level. The door to Victor Janovich's office looked medieval, the dark lumber several inches thick.

Fifteen minutes later, Kroodsma came outside to explain that no one at the office was expecting us, and it wasn't clear if there was a place for us to sleep at Victor Janovich's farm. "We're trying to call his assistant, but the phones aren't working half the time. We'll get it figured out." Kroodsma ducked back inside. A short while later, he came out of the building again and stood just outside the doorway. "I'm just going to let Julio handle this. Without Julio we'd be lost. He'll find a place for us to sleep." Moments later, though, Kroodsma went back inside and I could hear him talking with Julio, who was going from Spanish to English and back again every few seconds. No one had passed by on the street, so I walked to the threshold and peered in. The room, largely empty, looked more like a warehouse than an office, with one desk in the middle where Julio stood with a phone in his hand. Now, Javier confessed he didn't think there were any beds for us at the farmhouse. And he knew nothing about bellbirds in the area.

"Well, that changes things," Kroodsma said. "What should we do, Julio? Should we try La Selva Negra?" Kroodsma was referring to a tourist lodge less than an hour's drive away. Julio was concerned we would insult our host if we stayed somewhere else, but after a minute of indecision Kroodsma pulled out his notebook and located the phone number for La Selva Negra. Julio placed the call.

"They have a room," he said.

In the late 1990s, Chris Sharpe, a British birder, recorded birds in Nicaragua, including bellbirds here in the forests at La Selva Negra. No one knew, though, if the Nicaraguan bellbirds migrated as Monteverde birds did. No one knew much of anything about the Nicaraguan population. Kroodsma was mentally prepared to come back without any recordings. It was, therefore, a surprise to wake at 5 A.M. the following morning and find Kroodsma and Julio standing just outside the door, still in pajamas, debating who first heard the bellbird calling from the forest a hundred yards from our doorstep.

Kroodsma dressed hurriedly, grabbed his tape recorder, and stepped out the door, then stopped, realizing that, having arrived in darkness late last night, he had no sense of the terrain. In the dim light, we could see a forested slope to the north. "We need a map," Kroodsma said. "I wonder what time the office opens." He stood for a moment, looking around, then ignored his own question and set off on a path that led toward the calling bellbird. Two or three minutes later the path turned away from the bellbird, so Kroodsma headed into the forest, moving slowly through dense undergrowth. The sky brightened, but the sun remained behind a mountain slope. Julio pulled out his compass, but the bellbird's call, like a tolling buoy, determined Kroodsma's path. For twenty minutes we struggled through vines, then suddenly came out onto a trail leading up the mountain. We were close enough now to the bellbird that Kroodsma lifted his parabola and began taping. Danilo continued up the trail to try to get a look at the bird.

When a second bird began calling to the east, Kroodsma left to look for it while Julio continued to record the first bird. A few hundred yards away Danilo had found a sight line on the second bird, an adult with long wattles. So far Kroodsma had said little about what he'd heard, but when the bellbird flew off after several minutes, a smile spread over his face. He closed his eyes and slowly nodded his head as if affirming something we all agreed on. "These birds are entirely different. It's amazing. The bonk has a different tone, and it's shorter, and did you hear those soft sounds after it?" I could not hear them as well as Kroodsma, but I could tell they only vaguely resembled the whistles and swishing sounds of the Monteverde and Panama birds. There seemed to be several different calls, Kroodsma said. The one we were hearing most often began with a *bonk* and was followed by swishes, then a louder sound, then more swishes, and finally a whistle that rose and fell and rose again. The whistles were sweeter and more pleasing than those of the birds in Monteverde. There was also a call that began with a particularly loud *bonk* followed by a screech. Kroodsma was still categorizing and memorizing the calls. He also noticed that the bird's actions were different. It did not open its beak wide, then gulp air, its throat and chest muscles heaving. Instead, it opened its beak and sang almost immediately. The differences were greater than he'd expected. "Imagine if we had gone to Victor Janovich's farm last night instead of coming here," Kroodsma said. "We wouldn't be here for this moment. All the trouble we had last night was really a blessing in disguise."

• • •

Kroodsma and Julio spent the morning recording these two bellbirds and a third one that appeared. By noon, Kroodsma was satisfied. "I've gotten as much as I really need from these Nicaraguan birds," he said. "If I had to leave tomorrow, it would be okay." With no banded birds to track down, Kroodsma needed only a few good recordings of the Nicaraguan bellbirds to illustrate the third dialect. The Nicaraguan portion of the trip had only begun, but already it seemed to be coming to a close. It was anticlimactic. Once again the fieldwork was unpredictable.

It was a good thing the first morning went so well because the following days were not productive. The two Nicaraguan students, "Chepe" Zolotoff and Alejandra Martinez, arrived at La Selva Negra in a Jeep later that day, and Kroodsma spent much of the second morning helping them with their recording technique and doing little recording himself. On the afternoon of the second day we moved to Victor Janovich's farm, getting our first look at the countryside and the villages, which dampened our spirits for the remainder of the trip. We passed many people carrying buckets of water, some of them children, half-dressed, or naked. The region was suffering a drought. Some claimed it was because the forests had been cut down. The rivers and creeks had dried up, and people had given up on farming and left the land in the mountains for shanty-towns down along the main highway. Dozens of people were standing idly beside the road, many of them young or middle-aged men sitting on the ground and staring blankly ahead. "They are waiting to die," Javier, our driver, told us. People in this area were literally starving to death, he said. We felt uncomfortably conspicuous in a white SUV with tinted windows, and when people looked in our direction, their expressions didn't seem friendly. Javier warned us not to look directly at the women. The men were jealous, he said, and life was cheap; everyone carried a machete. It was hard to know how true this was, but we saw no smiles and many machetes. While we were guests of Victor Janovich, we would be accompanied on any trips into the forest by an armed guard.

The farm was less stately than we had imagined. The small house where we would stay was a simple stucco structure with fading paint and dull tile floors. The windows had battered wooden shutters that closed well enough perhaps to keep out small mammals. The rooms were bare except for a wooden table and two chairs. There was electricity, but not a bed in sight. Chepe and Alejandra had brought sleeping pads with them, and eventually we located three small, dirty mattresses. But there were four of us of course. We had been spoiled by our accommodations in Monteverde. By the time we brought our bags in, it was nearing dusk. Javier told us he had been instructed to take us tomorrow to Las Nubes, a new coffee plantation Janovich had established in the mountains a couple of hours from here. Bellbirds were common in the area, he said. Given all the confusion over our stay at the farm, we had doubts. Kroodsma was fast losing his usual optimism. "I wish I had more control over this situation," he said softly. "I'd like to know exactly where we are going and . . ." His voice trailed off.

We rose shortly after 4 A.M. to meet Victor Janovich's assistant, also named Victor, at a junction on the main highway from which he would lead the way to Las Nubes and the forest full of bellbirds. When we arrived at the meeting place, though, Victor Number Two wasn't there, and half an hour later he still hadn't shown up. We waited, walking along the edge of the highway, watching blue-black grassquits and gray-crowned yellowthroats forage in the long grasses. Kroodsma didn't let the delay trouble him: "Well, let's think about what we know about what's happening today. There are supposed to be bellbirds at Las Nubes, and we're late getting going, but we have all of the tapes we really need already. Today, we just smell the roses. We were lucky we went to La Selva Negra first. I began to get a helpless feeling as soon as we arrived at the farm yesterday."

After another half hour of waiting, we headed into Matagalpa to locate Victor Number Two, stopping first at the office, then driving to his house, where we found him coming out the door ready to begin the day. We set off, following him in his pickup truck, but within moments he pulled into a gas station, where, despite there being twice as many attendants as gas pumps, we spent a long twenty minutes. An hour and a half after we had left to search for Victor Number Two, we were back at the original meeting place on the highway. Now we turned north and started out for the bellbirds of Las Nubes. If Matagalpa was a poor town of the northern countryside, we were now headed into a region of cruel poverty. We drove for two hours along increasingly unstable roadbeds, sloshing through thick mud and streams. Even here, though, we saw the same yellow and blue sign that we had come across throughout Nicaragua, a government slogan: *Obra No Palabras,* or "Action, not words." The colorful signs were a sharp contrast to the shanties along the road, which looked as if they had been constructed by nine-year-olds. Some of the homes were nothing more than four walls, though *wall* doesn't seem like the right word for stakes set close together and pounded into the ground. Atop the stakes was a roof of miscellaneous sheets of metal or plastic. Black smoke poured out the openings. What, one wondered, could they be cooking?

It was nearly 10 A.M. by the time we reached Las Nubes. We rose slowly higher and higher into the mountains, and the final half mile was particularly steep and rough. Javier parked the four-wheel-drive Explorer, worrying that the vehicle wouldn't clear the rocks along the way. (Not until later did we realize the vehicle didn't belong to Victor Janovich; Javier had rented it before he picked us up at the airport.) We piled into the back of Victor Number Two's pickup truck, which bounced and slid up the slope, stopping at a small farmhouse. There we were introduced to our guide, a small, barefoot kid in shorts, sleeveless shirt, and a dirty green Nike baseball cap. He looked to be fifteen or sixteen years old. He would lead us to the bellbirds, we were told. A second man would accompany us, our guard, armed with a battered AK-47 with one clip of ammunition in the weapon and a second clip stuck in the front pocket of his torn blue jeans. Someone was robbed and murdered in these mountains not long ago. Bandits were in the area. Before we could decide how accurate this information was, our guide turned and headed toward the forest.

Many of the slopes surrounding Las Nubes were stripped bare and planted with crops, but to the north, primary forest rose up a steep ridge. We were inside the forest within a few minutes, following, in single file, the kid in the Nike cap, who swept a machete to clear the way. The vegetation was dense, and to minimize swinging the machete, our guide followed a streambed up the ridge. We stepped from rock to rock, crossing to one side of the stream, then the other, trying not to slip on the muddy banks. The slope quickly grew steeper, so we looked for handholds, grabbing at saplings and vines. Thinking of the thorn in Danilo's shin, I looked at each branch before I reached for it, while up ahead I could see our young leader moving nimbly up the ridge at a pace that concerned me. Vines ensnared our feet as we went, and more than once a thorn grabbed the cap off my head. Within minutes my forearms were streaked with scratches. Chepe and Alejandra seemed to have the least difficulty, and Javier was doing fine despite carrying a gallon jug of water in one hand. The streambed became increasingly slippery. We fell to our knees frequently, sliding backward a few feet before grabbing a branch. Near the top of the ridge, we moved away from the stream. I could hear the steady thwack of the machete but saw no real sign of a cleared path. It wouldn't occur to me until much later that our guide was a foot shorter than Kroodsma and me so the vines he ducked under caught us at neck level.

At the first ridgetop we walked on level ground for a short distance through broad-leaved grasses that grew over our heads, then we started up another slope. By now, perhaps twenty minutes into our hike, I was steadily panting and having trouble keeping up. Our footing was marginally better, but this was offset by how steep this slope was. In places it was nearly vertical. Each person stayed a few steps behind the other to avoid becoming a bowling pin if someone in front fell and slid backward. The line ahead of me stopped for a moment as Julio discussed with our guide which way to go. I gulped water between gulps of air, and then we were off again. When we reached the top of this second ridge, Julio called the procession to a halt. Through the trees we could see other ridges, so Julio put his parabola to his ear like a giant cupped hand to listen for bellbirds. Before we'd set out, he and Kroodsma were convinced there would be no bellbirds here. If there were, we would have heard them from the farmhouse. Kroodsma, in fact, had never taken his recorder out of his backpack. More discussion ensued, and our guide insisted that we needed to get to another ridge before we would find the bellbirds, so on we went, reaching an opening atop the next ridge. Once again we stopped. Someone thought this called for picture-taking, and as we posed for several group shots, Julio suggested Kroodsma pose with the AK-47. Our guard was happy to oblige, but before he handed the gun to Kroodsma, he placed the safety on, eliciting some alarm from those of us who, moments earlier, had been walking directly ahead of him up the slippery slopes.

Again Julio conferred with our guide about the elusive bellbirds of the area. There was talk of hiking around the other side of the ridge before us. We were getting close to the bellbirds, we were assured. We had not been gone long and giving up so soon would likely seem an insult, so we started off again. But ten minutes later, after we'd begun a steep descent, Julio and Kroodsma decided it was time to stop worrying about hurting someone's feelings and head back. Our guide looked around, decided on a direction, and resumed swinging his machete. Not ten minutes had gone by, however, before Julio questioned whether we were returning to the farmhouse and discovered we were not. There were bellbirds over the next ridge. Julio insisted again that we wanted to return to the farmhouse. We would take a shortcut back, we were told, but moments later we stopped to discuss which way to go, and our guide interpreted this to mean we might still want to look for the bellbirds. On and on this went. The descent to the farmhouse took longer than the ascent, and by the time we reached the porch of the small farmhouse, I collapsed. I sat in a chair, panting, my head spinning. Kroodsma sat down next to me. He looked tired also, but not concerned that we'd wasted a morning. "I wonder if the birds are ever in this area," he said. "It was sort of a wild-bellbird chase, wasn't it?"

After three years of recording, and with a suitcase of new tapes from Costa Rica at Julio's house, Kroodsma seemed to enjoy the notion of chasing imaginary bellbirds. The thought of a wild-bellbird chase stayed with me on the long ride back to Victor Janovich's farmhouse, and through the next two days as the trip came to an end.

A year later Kroodsma had not yet prepared a paper to support his assertion that the bellbird was learning its song, but in his mind he had the evidence lined up. First, clearly there were three dialects, and he had more than enough recordings to document this. Even a casual listener could tell the difference between the songs of Monteverde, Talamanca, and Nicaraguan birds. Sonograms of the recordings were concrete and unequivocal. In addition, sonograms illustrated that all the birds with the Monteverde dialect sang the three different Monteverde songs the same way with only the minor idiosyncrasies typical of birds with dialects. The same was true for the Talamanca singers, whether they were recorded near Monteverde or near the Costa Rica–Panama border, and also for the three Nicaraguan birds Kroodsma and Julio reported. By every commonly accepted principle in avian bioacoustics, this meant either the bellbird was learning its song or there were different species identical in every visible way. And the latter seemed far less likely when one considered all the other evidence.

The second important fact—juvenile bellbirds sang imperfect songs, developing the proper vocalizations over time just as young songbirds did—emerged early in Kroodsma's research, and it remained one of the most convincing aspects of the case.

The bellbird's song development mirrored the song-learning of oscines and was in sharp contrast to what had been observed with young suboscines, whose genetically inherited songs came out perfect and whole from the beginning. Here too Kroodsma had accumulated a substantial sampling of recordings to support the assertion. And because of the plumage changes in the first six years of a bellbird's life, which Debra Hamilton had documented with banded birds, Kroodsma could provide numerous sonograms of juvenile birds of known ages.

Third, he had a significant sampling of juvenile bellbirds that were combining elements of the Monteverde and Talamanca dialects—the "bilingual birds." This also was typical oscine song-learning behavior, occurring frequently among young songbirds living on the boundary of two dialects. By contrast, if the two dialects were genetically encoded and there were two species of bellbirds, some young birds would likely be a hybrid of the two species, in which case they would sing songs that were a Monteverde-Talamanca mixture. The hybrid songs would not include pure elements of the Monteverde and Talamanca dialects as did the bilingual singers Kroodsma recorded.

In addition to the evidence Kroodsma had compiled himself, there was the case of the bare-throated bellbird in Brazil that had learned blackbird vocalizations. Kroodsma knew from his talk at Rockefeller University in the spring of 2001 that his colleagues were eager to explain away each point in his case. Perhaps the slow development of the song was in the genes. Why wasn't that just as good an explanation and one that jibed with the accepted understanding that suboscines did not learn their songs? The same could be said for the bilingual songs of juvenile birds. Such reasoning, however, failed a standard scientific principle known as Occam's razor, which proposes that one should shave down the accumulation of possible explanations until the simplest reasonable explanation remains. It was possible to attribute the bellbird's singing behavior to something other than learning, but vocal learning was the simplest, most obvious explanation.

Besides, Kroodsma had a trump card.

When Kroodsma read Barbara Snow's description of the bellbird's vocalizations in the paper she published in 1977, he was surprised it didn't seem to quite match what the bellbirds sounded like to him. Fortunately, Snow had also recorded several of the birds and made sonograms. Kroodsma looked closely at the sonograms and discovered a number of distinct differences between the bellbirds in 1974 and the birds he was listening to twenty-five years later. Most notably, the frequency of the whistle was significantly higher in 1974 than it was now. What was going on? He considered the possibility that Snow's tape recorder was poorly calibrated or her sonograms carelessly prepared, but he knew from various sources that Barbara Snow was a diligent, respected researcher whose work could be trusted. No, he thought, Snow's recordings were accurate. The bellbirds had literally changed their tune.

The songs of mimics like mockingbirds and starlings change year to year, but the variation occurs within the repertoire of individual birds, which add new songs or new elements to old songs. An entire population of mockingbirds does not change the basic frequency of a shared song element. There are also documented cases of songs shared by a group of birds changing over time. Indigo buntings, for instance, live in small "neighborhoods" of, typically, three or four birds that share a unique version of the bunting's species song. Birds in an adjacent neighborhood all sing a different version. Because variations on the shared song may enter a neighborhood in various ways (a newcomer sticking to his own innovation rather than adapting to the neighborhood, for example), changes occur from generation to generation as birds with one song die and are replaced by young birds with the new song. Eventually, the unique song of a neighborhood has been replaced by a new one. This kind of change, however, occurs with small groups of birds, and for indigo buntings it takes on average ten years for a song to change entirely.

Early on, Kroodsma suspected something different was occurring with the bellbirds. He took into account that while the average life span of an indigo bunting is three years, the three-wattled bellbirds appear to live long lives. Some of the bellbirds that Barbara Snow studied in 1974 might still be around today. This led Kroodsma to think about other recordings that had been made of the bellbirds over the years. He gathered tapes from every source he could think of. Greg Budney sent him everything from the LNS archives. Kroodsma tracked down recordings from two biologists who'd worked in Monteverde in the mid-1980s and found tapes from the early 1990s too. He began making sonograms and looking closely at the frequency of the whistle in the Monteverde dialect. Although he saw at least a dozen other elements that were changing, the whistle was easiest to measure, and it came through clearly on every recording.

Studying the sonograms, he calculated that the average frequency of the whistle in Snow's 1974 recordings was 5,580 hertz. When he did the same calculation for other years, he was stunned by the results. In 1981, the average frequency was 4,620 hertz. In 1991, it was 4,405. In 1999, Kroodsma's first year of recording, it was 3,782. The frequency was falling, dropping an average of 72 hertz per year. This was the strangest thing Kroodsma had ever come across. Hardly believing what he had uncovered, he looked next at his own recordings and saw that the frequency was still dropping each year. By the end of the study, he could document a steady decline in frequency. Furthermore, from his relentless pursuit of banded birds, Kroodsma could illustrate this changing frequency in an individual bellbird—Azul/Oro–Oro/Azul, a bird

George Powell had originally banded in 1994 when it was three years old. In 1999, as an eight-year-old, its whistle occurred at 3,771 hertz, very near the average of 3,782 hertz for all birds that year. Kroodsma found Azul/Oro–Oro/Azul again in 2000. His whistle had dropped to 3,724 hertz.

In effect, the bellbirds were either agreeing on a new song each year or continually changing the agreed-upon song, each bird changing his song to match the others. This could not be hardwired in the bird's genes, Kroodsma reasoned. It must be a result of birds listening to each other and changing the song. No other songbird did anything like this. It was, Kroodsma said, as if someone had perpetrated a giant hoax. There was nothing like it. Or, more accurately, there was nothing else like it in the bird world. There was, however, one animal that did something similar—the humpback whale.

Whales and other cetaceans are the only other animals on Earth that learn their vocalizations. Though one cannot duplicate with whales the kind of laboratory experiments that have been done with birds, all the available evidence suggests whales learn their songs. One of the best indications comes from researchers listening to humpback whales. During their breeding season, male humpback whales sing a long, complex song that appears to help maintain an established distance between individuals. The humpback whales in the Atlantic Ocean all sing a shared song, as do the humpbacks in the Pacific Ocean. Throughout the breeding season the song changes as some phrases are dropped and others are replaced by new phrases. As the changes occur, all the whales make the necessary adjustments so that they continue to sing one distinctive humpback whale song. When the whales disperse after the breeding season and return half a year later, they remember where they left off, picking up the song as it was when last sung the previous year.

This odd couple—whales and bellbirds—share something else

that fascinates Kroodsma because it may be linked to the great mystery of how song-learning evolved in birds. During breeding season, male humpback whales form groups in floating territories and sing for hours. They are auditioning for females, some believe, creating a fierce competition in which the males' singing prowess influences their mating success. Those males that sing the best version of the shared song may receive the affections of more than one female, leaving many males without mating opportunities. This mating scenario is, of course, similar to the dispersed leks of the three-wattled bellbird. Kroodsma believes the competition in leks gives unsuccessful males an incentive to learn the species song. Perhaps, Kroodsma says, it is the older, more successful males that make changes in the song from year to year, and the younger animals, whether whales or bellbirds, follow their lead. Add to this the case of the little hermit, a neotropical hummingbird that displays in leks. In a much cited paper, "The Origins of Vocal Learning," Fernando Nottebohm summarizes the little hermit's behavior: "Each male has a song theme closely resembling that sung by surrounding neighbors. Different clusters of birds within the same singing assembly have different song themes, while birds in other assemblies have still others. . . . [Most] likely, young males settling in a display ground imitate songs of neighbors."

Could it be that the intense competition between males performing in leks leads to song-learning? Is this the story the three-wattled bellbird is telling? "I feel like I'm on quicksand here," says Kroodsma. "To be on more solid ground I'd like to know more about the other cotingas, their genealogy. It would help to know which species is the closest living relative of the bellbird and what its mating system is. We know so little about any of these birds. And we're a long ways from having the relative relationships of the cotingas worked out so that you can plot them all on an evolutionary tree. We're talking about another few lifetimes of work."

Will the bellbird still be around a few decades from now? From Costa Rica the most recent news is mixed. The Monteverde bellbird population is clearly in decline, and there is no reason to believe this will change anytime soon. One cannot reverse the habitat loss on the Pacific slope overnight. Protecting the land that remains is the priority, and here there is a bit of good news. In the years since Kroodsma's 2001 recording trip, Debra Hamilton and others have established the Fundación Conservacionista Costarricense, The Costa Rica Conservation Foundation, with the principal goal of saving the bellbird. Hamilton, director of the foundation, has raised funds from individuals, student groups, and other organizations to purchase land where the bellbirds often congregate after the breeding season. In January 2003, the foundation made a down payment on eleven hectares of forest. When I spoke to Hamilton in August of 2003, she was particularly pleased that the bellbird was getting more attention than it had in the past. A month earlier, the foundation had hosted a visit by Costa Rica's minister of the environment and two dozen members of the Costa Rican Ornithological Society, led by Julio Sanchez. The bellbird was the topic of the day, and the event was covered on television. And yet, as the foundation struggled to come up with enough money to make the next payment on the land, it was clear that its limited funds could not cover everything at once: Hamilton had to cancel the bellbird census for 2003.

In January of 2003, I met Kroodsma in south Florida. He had not yet written his paper on the bellbirds. He had no sense of urgency about telling the scientific community that a suboscine—contrary to all that was known about birdsong—was learning its song. I shouldn't have been surprised, but I was. The passion that drove his fieldwork appeared to be swallowed by a profound ambivalence he felt toward the scientific profession and careerism. Ever restless, he had begun working on a book on birdsong for the general reader and was planning a cross-country bicycle trip with his son for the summer of 2003. He and his son would ride from Virginia to Oregon. "We leave on a Friday," Kroodsma told me. "We'll start out hearing Carolina chickadees, then as we head up and over the Shenandoah Mountains, we'll listen for black-capped chickadees and the hybrid songs where the two species meet. We'll be traveling through chickadee song zones all the way to Oregon." Kroodsma did not imagine that he would do more work on the bellbird. He would leave it to others. "Some people might throw stones at me for not settling down." He laughed at the image. "But I can catch those stones."

It was, in the end, all a kind of wild-bellbird chase. And it was the chase that mattered, the pursuit of order and understanding, a life spent adding pieces to a puzzle that will never be complete.

ACKNOWLEDGMENTS

Don Kroodsma shared his life's work with me over the course of nearly ten years. I am deeply grateful to him for his generosity, good companionship in travel, and the many hours he spent patiently explaining avian bio-acoustics to me. Greg Budney's passion for birdsong and recording set this book in motion. My great thanks to him for talking with me at the Macaulay Library of Natural Sounds and for our time together in the field. And many thanks also to Debra Hamilton for her warm hospitality in Costa Rica and her expertise on the three-wattled bellbird. Much of what is known about the three-wattled bellbird comes from the important work she and others have done.

My days in the field in Costa Rica would not have been so rewarding and pleasurable were it not for the good company of Julio Sanchez, Danilo Brenes, and Dave Stemple. Others in Costa Rica were very helpful, including George Powell, Marcony Suarez, and Terri Mallory. Thanks as well to Melissa Kroodsma for her good company and for providing me with photographs that helped jog my memory. The trip to Nicaragua would not have been possible without the aid of Victor Janovich, "Chepe" Zolotoff, and Alejandra Martinez.

The co-leaders of the 2001 LNS Sound Recording Workshop—David Herr, Randy Little, and Kathy Dunsmore—played a far larger role at the workshop than my account suggests. Their wide-ranging knowledge of birdsong, recording, and analysis of sounds appears uncredited in several places. I have many good memories from a week of sunrises with the 2001 workshop participants: Eduardo Bejerano, Adele Binning, Michael Brezin, Susannah Buhrman, Frank Dorritie, Laura Erickson, Ashley Hayes, Santiago Imberti, Gadi Katzir, Christin Khan, Richard Peet, Nick Plavac, Carmen Salsbury, Tamara Smyth, Richard Tkachuck, and Paul Voigt. My grati-

ACKNOWLEDGMENTS

tude also to Greg Clark; Geoff Keller; Jim Steele; and, from National Public Radio, Carolyn Jensen (who graciously provided me with transcripts from NPR's recordings at the workshop), Alex Chadwick, Sean Fox, and Bill McQuay. And I have not forgotten the helpful talk on physics and sound waves I had one afternoon with Bob Grotke. My appreciation as well to John Fitzpatrick, director of the Cornell Laboratory of Ornithology, and Jack Bradbury, director of the Macaulay Library of Natural Sounds, for their important work.

Special thanks to Peter Marler, Robert Dooling, and Alan Feduccia for taking time to talk with me about their work.

I worked with several editors on articles related to *Birdsong* that fed this book. My thanks to Roger Cohn, Pat Crow, David Seideman, Michael Robbins, and Jennifer Bogo at *Audubon*, and Tim Gallagher at *Living Bird*. At Scribner, Beth Wareham's insightful editing was invaluable, and thanks to Nan Graham for her belief in this project, and also to Rica Allannic and Susan Moldow. John Taylor Williams's enthusiasm for this book and expert guidance have been a source of great comfort, as has the warm voice and attention to detail of Hope Denekamp.

I am particularly grateful to Stuart Dybek for countless bits of advice and for reading the manuscript at various stages. His comments on a late draft were especially helpful. And many thanks to Tracy Kidder for his careful reading of the manuscript and his suggestions.

Finally, I am deeply grateful to Terry Thaxton for her support and help with the manuscript from beginning to end.

A special note: Thanks to Don Kroodsma and Houghton-Mifflin for permission to include excerpts from Kroodsma's forthcoming book *The Singing Life of Birds*.

Throughout the manuscript I have often referred to the Macaulay Library of Natural Sounds simply as LNS, which is how I came to know the institution originally. Information on LNS is available at its website: http://www.birds.cornell.edu/macaulaylibrary/.

INDEX

INDEX